Richard **Burns**

Also by this author:

COLIN McRAE
Rallying's fast master

Richard Burns

Rallying's would-be king by David Williams

Foreword by Tommi Mäkinen

© David Williams 2000

First published in November 2000

British Library Cataloguing in Publication Data:
A catalogue record for this book is available from the British Library

ISBN 1 85960 687 3

Library of Congress catalog card no. 00-134242

Haynes North America, Inc.
861 Lawrence Drive, Newbury Park,
California 91320, USA

Previous page: Safari 2000. (McKlein)

Haynes Publishing, Sparkford, Nr Yeovil, Somerset, BA22 7JJ.
Tel: 01963 442030 Fax: 01963 440001
Int. tel: +44 1963 442030 Fax: +44 1963 440001
E-mail: sales@haynes-manuals.co.uk
Web site: www.haynes.co.uk

Designed & typeset by G&M, Raunds, Northamptonshire, England
Printed and bound in England by J.H. Haynes & Co. Ltd, Sparkford

Contents

Acknowledgements

Prone to sins of omission as they are, acknowledgements can be unusually gratifying to the author too. In this instance, so many people have unstintingly offered their time and assistance that space may run short.

First and foremost, I should express my gratitude to Richard and the Burns family. I am also in debt to Keith Baud, 'Possum' Bourne, Amanda Campbell, Andrew Cowan, Bertie Fisher, Jerry Freeman, Mike and Sue Greasley, Gordon Jarvis, Belinda Jellett, John King, David Llewellin, Bernard Lindauer, Alister McRae, Andy Moss, Maggie Railton, Robert Reid, Peter Rushforth, Mick Shonfield, Phil Short, Saffron Small, Mervyn Wheeler, David Williams and Malcolm Wilson. It is perhaps worth emphasising at this point that all the references in the text to David Williams are to Richard's old friend and mentor, not to the author; we are not related.

It would be impossible to name everyone at Prodrive who provided anecdotes, assessment and, in some cases, photographs, but I will single out Simon Cole, David Lapworth and David Richards.

I'm grateful to Mark Hughes, Flora Myer, Peter Nicholson, Darryl Reach and Alison Roelich at Haynes Publishing for their unstinting professionalism and tolerance of awkward deadlines. Photographically, Mark Griffin, Gavin Lodge and above all, the McKlein trio – Colin McMaster, Bob McCaffrey and Reinhard Klein himself – have offered sterling support. I must also thank Neil Randon for allowing me to scour the archives at *Motoring News*. Pictures not otherwise credited come from the personal collection of the Burns family.

Foreword by Tommi Mäkinen

World Rally Champion 1996–1999

Like most Finnish rally drivers, I first went to Britain when I was quite young, so I met Richard Burns so long ago that I don't remember it! We were driving quite different sorts of cars in those early days in the British Championship and I think the first time I really remember him as a driver was when I was with Mitsubishi and he was like the junior driver for Subaru.

The first time that I saw his true performance was when we were against each other on the Thailand Rally in 1995. He was driving with Subaru that year and his performance was excellent – although I think I won!

Then the year after that we became team-mates at Mitsubishi for the World and the Asia-Pacific Championships. He was a very good, easy team-mate. It was never any problem – there was not at all any opposition between us, which can happen sometimes.

I don't think I taught him so much, because our driving styles are so different, so we could discuss things about the car together, but what was good for me wasn't always good for him. In the end, we drove quite similar cars even though our styles are so different. His co-driver Robert Reid came in a rally car with me, but I don't think Richard ever did.

I was following his way to learn things

though, because it was quite different from most drivers. It was actually quite a good way to do it. He started a bit carefully. He took his time to learn the car, learn the stages, learn the rallies. He took his time the first year, improving every day until he found his full confidence. There are so many drivers who do things in a different way and just keep going flat out until they have an accident. I remember from the start I was pushing very hard, so it was a little bit different, but Richard had a very good way to learn and of course, by the time he left Mitsubishi, he had won two World Championship rallies.

We are not especially close friends, but that is quite normal. It is quite a hard life travelling all the time, so although it is good to see other drivers, all of us have our own lives and our own friends. Also, we are opponents, so it is a bit hard to be really friendly. It's quite natural after the rally that we want to be immediately somewhere else, completely out from the rally. You don't want to see the same faces all the time!

Now of course, Richard is at the level where a true World Championship driver has to be. He is doing very well. It is difficult to know what he can do in future. He is on the right level for a World Champion, but rallying is not predictable and things can go up and down, so you don't always get the results you think you deserve. But I think now everyone can agree there is no question that he has the ability.

Introduction

It takes a great deal to attract Cardiff's attention on the day of an international rugby match, but on 26 November 2000 the Welsh capital swivelled its gaze and paid homage to an Englishman. As Richard Burns drove on to the finish ramp of the Rally of Great Britain, the crowd burst into applause and sounded klaxons in a noisy tribute to an extraordinary performance. He had won the rally for the third year in a row, a feat last attained 25 years previously by one of the sport's legends, Timo Mäkinen. It was too early to talk of legendary status perhaps, but Richard had earned not just the plaudits of the crowd, but an even scarcer commodity, the respect of the Finns.

Richard Burns is an unlikely rally dri-

Corsica used to be nicknamed the 'rally of the 10,000 corners'. It was scarcely an exaggeration. (McKlein)

ver. The most successful tend to have a background in the motor trade or in farming and there is a good chance of a previous family involvement in the sport too. Richard was born and brought up in the prosperous heart of southern England, in the countryside perhaps, but in a densely populated part of it where space is at a premium and there are no major rallies. It is a long way from the sport's British heartlands in the north and west. He never stood beside a forest track as a small boy watching the RAC Rally hurtle past, and there were no old cars to tinker with, or fields in which to learn the essence of car control.

Yet the fascination with cars was present from the start. He began driving in the Under 17s Car Club and once he discovered rallying, nothing was going to prevent Burns from trying to become a rally driver himself. At that point, the World Championship was scarcely a dream, far less a goal. The prospect of being able to drive a rally car was sufficient reward in itself. He was lucky that motorsport runs deep at amateur level in Britain and that he met people who were able and willing to help him in his formative years. He has a knack of getting people on his side, in fact. The boyish enthusiasm is less evident now, but the dedication has never wavered. Richard was prepared to do whatever it took, from scratching a living by stacking supermarket shelves or driving delivery vans, to working on his fitness or improving his mechanical skills. Knuckling down to a career would have been an admission of failure.

Nothing came easily. Those close to him were won over by his skill as much as his attitude, but the outside world sometimes perceived him – quite unfairly – as a rich and privileged young man who rarely got dirt under his fingernails. The feeling was that while he was able and presentable, he lacked the raw talent to make the grade. In a perverse way, his all-round capability made him appear too much the finished article when he was still in his teens. As some of his supporters acknowledged, his early successes seemed to trigger suspi-

cion and approbation in roughly equal proportions. Beyond question, the winning manner as an individual failed to turn him into a people's hero overnight.

It wasn't just Richard's background that was unusual, but his technique. Crashing is a feature of any form of motorsport, but in rallying it occasionally seems to be an inseparable part of the process: the rugged nature of the terrain plays its part, aggression is vital and there are no marks lost on major rallies for panel damage these days. Burns has never been at ease with that approach. It is impossible to imagine him describing a roll as the quickest, safest way to stop, as the 1984 World Champion Stig Blomqvist nonchalantly did when driving for Saab. On the contrary, Burns seemed almost to recoil from taking risks. He once daringly told an interviewer that he was an artist – like any driver.

Burns's meticulously planned, carefully paced, utterly disciplined style invited the charge that he lacked the stomach for hand to hand combat. Despite the electrifying speed at which he ascended the rungs in British rallying – for the comparative lack of accidents never interrupted a steady stream of success – there was an assumption that each championship won merely brought him closer to his level of incompetence. By the time he was 23, he had won a major rally championship four years running, twice in Peugeots, then twice in Subarus.

After he became a factory driver with Subaru, it seemed for a time as though his detractors might be correct. His form and self-confidence faltered. To an extent, the critics might be forgiven for misjudging him, for he is nothing if not a contradictory figure. Professionally, he is detached to the point of coldness, yet he is also intensely status-conscious, something of a fashion-struck city boy in a countryman's sport. He does not enjoy travelling, yet is rarely in one place for more than a few days at a time. He is shrewd enough to

Concentration is the name of the game at this level of rallying. (McKlein)

Imprezas are designed with rallying in mind and Richard has played his full part in turning them into cult cars. (McKlein)

know that seeing the world primarily through a windscreen is bound to be superficial and that there is nothing glamorous about living in a succession of hotel rooms. Above all, he relishes the chance to take on Colin McRae, but resents the constant, inescapable comparison.

Burns has good reason to believe that comparisons are odious. McRae has done him a favour to the extent that the Scot's whirlwind rise shattered the prejudice that British rally drivers were irretrievably second rate, but the disadvantages are more apparent. Burns did not demonstrate McRae's instant turn of speed and he rarely displays quite the same crowd-pleasing manner at the wheel. Fans do not warm to an accumulator in the way that they thrill to a driver who appears to treat each corner as if it were his last. Burns has suffered both from being younger and less seasoned, and from the outside world's failure to appreciate the importance of the equipment and experience in such a highly technical sport. In this environment an

apprenticeship can be an exasperating, infuriating thing, a sentence as much as an opportunity.

But latterly, Burns's dedication and patience have been rewarded. Turned loose by Subaru at the end of 1995, he was given the chance to find his feet at Mitsubishi. After a shaky start he rewarded the team with two World Championship rally victories in 1998 and played a key role in bringing it the manufacturers' world title. He could no longer be dismissed as a brittle understudy. Since returning to Subaru and replacing the take-no-prisoners Scot, he has become a respected lead driver and genuinely, by McRae's admission, an equal. The styles may contrast and Burns was horrified at the fleeting prospect of McRae rejoining him at Subaru for 2001, but the mounting tally of World Championship rally wins speaks for itself. Burns is one of the handful of rally drivers whom any team manager would mortgage the factory to sign. He has all the credentials to become one of the sport's legends, a champion fit to stand comparison with Carlos Sainz, Walter Röhrl or Miki Biasion – the men who not only out-drove, but out-thought their opponents.

chapter one

The child prodigy

It was not an idyllic childhood, but it was comfortable enough. Born on 17 January 1971, Richard Burns was brought up in the attractive, wooded countryside west of London near his birthplace of Reading. When he was eight, the family moved from Stoke Row to an old farmhouse near Checkendon. There was more space, with stables for the horses kept by his mother, Denise. Richard, the younger child, was free to ride his bicycle around the yard and nearby country lanes.

But he hated school, hated team games, hated children's parties. The food was always sausages, chips and beans, and Richard disliked all of them. At school, he showed some aptitude for science-biased subjects and technical drawing – he has always had an eye for detail – and did enough work to pass six O-levels without the least display of enthusiasm, but he was a lonely, diffident boy, with few friends.

Cars were his consuming interest, to the extent that he could identify them passing the house, purely by sound. He begged for any chance to steer as soon as he was old enough to see over the wheel while sitting on his father's lap. Alex Burns, a Newcastle-born computer systems project manager, had ridden motorcycles during National Service in the Royal Marines and had carried out a little

necessary maintenance on the family's cars, but there was no other history of family involvement in motoring, Richard's parents assumed his interest was a schoolboy fad, until he requested a subscription to the racing and rallying weekly, *Motoring News*.

'On reflection – hindsight is a wonder-

Too young for wheels at nine months, Richard plays in the garden with his sister, Joanna.

ful thing – when did Richard become really interested in cars and driving? I think the answer is from the day he could recognise a car,' his father has suggested.

Richard had a voracious appetite for motoring magazines of any kind, in fact, but his life changed for good when he came across an article in the *Mail on Sunday* about the Under 17s Car Club. The club is, most emphatically, not designed as a school for budding rally drivers. It is intended to be an outlet for children who are keen on cars and wish to learn to drive under adult supervision, with a view to turning them into responsible, competent motorists, more than capable of passing the driving test. The requirements are that they should be big enough to reach the pedals and see through the windscreen, but be under 15 years of age when they join.

The Under 17s Car Club transformed Richard's life. He is seen at the wheel of his mother's Alfasud at the Harrow Driving Centre.

Alex wondered if Richard might be put off by his first meeting with the formidable instructor, Rob Blacker, but any misgivings were soon overcome. From the age of 11, Richard no longer made do with occasional drives in fields or birthday visits to garages. He lived for those weekends when there was an Under 17s meeting. The reluctant schoolboy shuffling sleepily to Gillotts comprehensive school during the week would spring from his bed at 7 o'clock on a Sunday morning, eager to be the first there so that he could spend as much time driving as possible.

There were between 20 and 25 meetings per year, at venues ranging from Finmere, a disused airfield north of Oxford, to the police driving school at Harrow and race tracks such as Castle Combe, Thruxton and Silverstone. The children got a chance to drive anything. Ostensibly, they drove their parents' cars, which meant that Richard variously used a Triumph 2000, an Alfasud or a Vauxhall Cavalier, but the club was able to borrow

all kinds of vehicles from manufacturers, ranging from Seddon Atkinson lorries to a Lotus Esprit. Richard kept a neatly written list of the cars he had tried. It included everything from a Metro 1.0L – that attention to detail again – to a Porsche 911 Cabrio.

He covered an astonishing mileage. On a good weekend, he might drive anything between 150 and 200 miles and, by the time he was finally licensed to drive on the road, he was already an accomplished, experienced driver, who had sampled a range of machinery fit to send the average learner goggle-eyed.

His gift for handling anything with wheels was apparent at once. He was the Under 17s CC's 'Driver of the Year' for the first time in 1984, when he was 13, retained his trophies in 1985 and won further awards in 1986. The competitive element consisted of driving tests against the clock, but they were primarily tests of manoeuvrability.

'There were things like skill tests and what have you and I don't think I've ever seen him take a wrong route. You have all these cones and I don't know about you, all I can see is a fog of cones. I've never seen him go wrong,' Alex recalled.

However, tests of manoeuvrability do not figure highly in Richard's memory of the Under 17s.

'I used to have a whale of a time at the weekends when I was driving and it used to be really quite free. My dad was chairman for a couple of years. He was always on the committee. It was like a social thing for both of us. We used to be some of the first people there in the morning and set up all the cones and stuff, and I used to mess around so badly. It was handbrake turns everywhere and flicking the car around everywhere – out of sight of all the parents and so on,' he said.

The most memorable car he drove was

The Under 17s CC fulfilled a car-mad schoolboy's wildest dreams. Richard was just about big enough to drive this turbocharged Esprit.

When it came to his driving test, Richard almost failed for going too slowly. In fact, he had already shown that he was capable of sustaining very much higher speeds and driving much quicker cars.

a Sierra Cosworth – not exactly the ideal thing for driving tests. It is worth pointing out that he never put so much as a scratch on a car at an Under 17s' event, but he did manage his first accident well before taking his test.

'He was practising his skidding and there was a patch of ice there and he skidded into the chicken shed. He came in absolutely crying his eyes out. I thought he'd killed one of the cats or something. It was ages before I got out of him that all he'd done was prang the car,' Alex said.

Driving did not confer popularity at school. Hardly anyone believed that a schoolboy could drive on a race track, let alone in a Porsche or a Lotus, so Richard learnt to keep his experiences to himself.

'I did lots of things that lots of teenagers didn't like or couldn't be – lots of things different. If there was ever a fad

going round school, that you had to have this personal stereo, I was like, "Well, why?" I had an air rifle for three years and then suddenly air rifles were the trendiest thing to have in school, so you had to go and get one. I'd had one for three years, so what's so interesting about that? I didn't follow fads particularly,' he said.

Driving did not necessarily find much favour with Denise though. She endured a few laps of Castle Combe once with her son driving a Capri 2.8 at a speed well in excess of what she regarded as suitable. She made her views plain to both Alex and Richard, and has not sat next to her son in a competitive environment since. She dutifully attends the Rally of Great Britain, but while she is proud of her son's achievements, she admits that she has never developed a taste for 'traipsing into a forest, up to your knees in mud, to watch cars so drenched in dirt that they're hardly identifiable.'

That is not to say that she disapproved of Richard's interest in cars. His parents recognised that there was no sense in attempting to disapprove, in trying to interest him in much else, or in suggesting that he might pursue a career in another field. Besides, Denise acknowledges that it had its practical side.

'He would have been about 12 or 13. I used to take Joanna, his sister, to horse-riding competitions and when we got to this one, it was about a two-acre field which was the parking for the whole competition, and I got to the gate and this man said, "Would you like to go and back that trailer into that little space over there?"

'I said, "I can't". And Richard said, "Oh, get out mum, I'll do it". So he did. And the person behind me saw him and came up and said, "Would you do mine?" And he spent the whole day parking people's trailers for them in these tiny spaces and that was the only horse event he ever enjoyed going to. He had a wonderful day.'

Although Richard and Alex had been spectating on a handful of local rallies, the sport does not have a massive following in the Home Counties and there was no particular focus to the son's interest in cars until a young man called Martin, who worked on his car in one of the Burns's sheds, mentioned going to a rally school.

Richard was captivated with the idea of trying something different and his father duly arranged a trip to Jan Churchill's Welsh Forest Rally School near Newtown.

This was a great deal easier said than done. The trip was a 15th birthday present and Churchill was far from captivated with the request. After much persuasion, special insurance was arranged and Richard – and Martin – got their hands on the school's Escort for a day.

From that moment on, Richard Burns knew what he wanted to do. There were no precise goals even then, no aim to become World Champion (the idea of a British World Rally Champion was almost as fanciful at the time as a British downhill ski champion) but he knew he wanted to drive rally cars.

This, at least, was not an unrealistic goal. Churchill, a well-regarded driver with a string of good results in Porsches behind him, reckoned that Richard was one of only two pupils he had had with real talent.

It did not take Richard long to work out that there were all kinds of ways of getting involved in rallying before his

Richard was prepared to help out in the stables, but horses were never his favourite animals.

Richard got used to winning prizes early in the Under 17s CC, but remained bashful when it came to making speeches. He has just received an award from the racing driver Barrie Williams at Barry in 1985.

17th birthday. He badgered his father into letting him join Craven Motor Club in Reading. People remember a gangling ginger-haired boy turning up at the club's weekly meetings at Old Redingensians' Rugby Club (a breezeblock construction as solid and stylish as a second-row forward) and showing them pictures of the cars he had driven. It was not long before he was doing odd jobs on Saturday mornings in the garages owned by club members such as Keith Edwards and Beric Ewan, working at Churchill's rally school during the holidays and helping marshal or service on local rallies. Richard was persuasive and nothing was too menial provided he was involved.

'Either people felt sorry for me or they did it just to get me off their backs. Looking back – I probably still do it with some things – people do help me out an extraordinary amount, way beyond what they're duty-bound to do and I don't know for the life of me why they do it, but I appreciate now what a little burden I was!' he reflected.

By the time he was 16, he had also had an experience that might have put him off rallying for good. In February 1987, he was marshalling at the finish of a stage of the Longleat Rally and was an eyewitness to a savage accident in which Steve Whiteford's co-driver, Dave Adams, was killed instantly. Whiteford was a successful amateur driver with a Metro 6R4 – pretty much the quickest car available to a privateer at the time.

The accident took place at a fork. Richard thinks that he was 'too young' to appreciate the gravity of it, but in any case, he rationalises what happened, as competition drivers often do.

'He must just have misheard or had his eyes looking down the left side – it must have been deceptive – and at the last minute he saw the cars parked down there and went to the right, and it was too late. He hit the grass, which was just a rise, and then he flew sideways, straight into the tree. I was standing like 200 metres away at the stop. It was weird, because he was just sitting there. His helmet had flown off out of the window and he was just sat in the car.'

Whiteford was also in the car, unconscious. For such a brutal crash, it sounds curiously peaceful.

Richard had discovered that RAC rules

permitted him to navigate and Alex himself was nagged into becoming a rally driver on road rallies – navigational events run at night, although there was a distinct performance element to most of them at the time. The fact that Alex was sufficiently level-headed not to pile the Cavalier into the first available hedge no doubt helped, but they achieved some respectable results, including third overall on one local event. Richard is engagingly modest about his map-reading abilities, however.

It was not entirely straightforward. Richard navigated other people too. He recalls bruising his knees when a less attentive driver careered through a stone wall in the Cotswolds and having to telephone his father to be rescued at 4 o'clock one Sunday morning.

The other drivers had included another Craven member, Gordon Jarvis, who had gone out of his way to foster Richard's enthusiasm. Richard had jumped at the chance to co-drive on a stage event and they finished 15th on a forest rally on the Berkshire–Surrey border in a 2-litre Sunbeam. A Coventry stalwart of a motor trader who had seen the company metamorphose from the Rootes Group to Chrysler, Talbot and Peugeot, Jarvis had rallied everything from Imps to Rapiers and Sunbeams, winning his class in the 1981 British Open Championship. One of those people who seems born to be a pillar of the community – he is rarely seen without a tie – it was natural to turn to him when Richard wanted a car of his own.

The original plan had been to buy an Escort, but all the available cars cost at least £800 and were in a dreadful state of repair. Jarvis, who worked at Reading Garage, found a £400 Sunbeam. It was an immaculate automatic and just the thing for a prudent daughter rather than a rally-mad son in Alex's estimation. Instead, it became Richard's 16th birthday present and he had a year to turn it into a rally car.

If it had wheels, Richard found a way of driving it – even a Seddon Atkinson lorry. Vehicle manufacturers and importers were more than willing to oblige the Under 17s CC.

Richard got his first chance to drive a rally car at the age of 15. It was a day that changed his life.

Enthusiasm ran ahead of experience. Told that the first task was to burn the underseal off, Richard soon got to work with a blowtorch, burning his wrists as hot underseal dripped from the floorpan. Professional help was obtained to weld the bodyshell where necessary and to repaint it, but the bulk of the work was carried out by the Burnses, father and son, and by Jarvis. Following the Longleat accident, the car's roll cage incorporated door bars from the outset.

Richard also displayed an aptitude for autotests. As manoeuvrability is the prime requirement and a speed in excess of 40mph on any test is good going, they are considered the preserve of Minis and Caterham-derived sports cars such as Duttons. There was general astonishment when a schoolboy driving his father's Cavalier proved capable not just of winning his class, but achieving top-five overall results too.

'He'd just sit on the start line, all cool, calm and collected, no revving of the engine or anything: five-four-three-two-one and he'd just go, wouldn't hit a thing and come back with fastest time. Then he'd hop out of the car and go back to whatever he was doing before – which was even more annoying, because he didn't seem to have to think about it. He'd be messing about before he got in the car and messing about when he got out of the car,' Alex explained. Richard knew he was causing a stir, but could not see quite what all the fuss was about.

'It was weird, because it was kind of what we'd been doing on a tighter scale at the Under 17s. They were just called driving tests: it was against the clock, but the cones were set so it was only three inches either side and six inches either end. An autotest was like that, but less restricted. I'd been doing it for ages in my old man's Cavalier, but of course they were all driving rally cars and things, which in some ways are not as good as a standard car to do that kind of thing.'

There was growing evidence that the boy was good. Alex and Denise had no means of being sure, but people who did, such as Churchill and Jarvis, assured them that Richard had genuine ability. It remained an unlikely basis for a career, however, and once he had passed his O-levels, Richard was given a choice. Either he went to college in Henley to study engineering, in which case he would have parental support for rallying, or he could skip any grounding for a career and any support for his rallying either. With considerable reluctance, he agreed to another two years of formal education.

chapter two

Clubbing together

Richard Burns was unlikely to flunk. He passed the exams and got his BTEC in general engineering, but a decade later, his opinion of his teachers at Henley still borders on the venomous.

'How much work did I do for it? Oh man, I used to eat pizza the whole time in the lessons and get told off for it. We used to have such rotten teachers as well – dreadful. I used to get hauled up so many times. I got chucked out or bollocked for not being there on Fridays, because I'd be going away on a rally. I remember so vividly being taken outside by our class tutor. He used to give me lectures on getting a proper job, engineering is a sound base and all the blah-blah-blah, and I bet he's still there, banging on.

'A lot of people used to say, "You're wasting your time, you've got to concentrate on this,' and there was only one decent teacher there. He was like general studies. He used to do stuff with businesses and banks. It was more like life than the rest of it. He was a really cool bloke. He was the only one who was keen and enthusiastic, and was actually encouraging. I'm afraid the education system didn't do an awful lot for me. I learnt a hell of a lot more about life going away on rallies than I ever did at school or at college.'

Much as it might grieve Richard to admit it, the college staff may have had a case. There was not much sign at that point that a career as a works rally driver lay just over the horizon. It was not that he lacked promise – quite the opposite – more that rallying offers not so much a ladder of opportunity as a slough of despond. There are no hurdles dependent on ability, no obvious equivalent of a racing category such as Formula Ford for the ambitious and the gifted – not at that time anyway – and no talent scouts. Consequently, stars do not necessarily shine. Skill is a prerequisite, but so are abnormal levels of perseverance, financial support and luck.

> **His partner was a calm dentist who also paid most of the costs**

As Richard's 17th birthday was on a Sunday, he had to wait another 24 hours before passing his driving test, although he nearly failed for going too slowly. That was not a problem once he started rallying the lovingly rebuilt Sunbeam.

The more enthusiastic Craven Motor Club members have stickers on their cars bearing the words 'Team Craven' and in Richard's case, that was entirely appropriate. As Richard's were too rusty, Beric Ewan loaned some doors and Jarvis did not take much persuading to lend his fully tuned 1600Ti engine and gearbox in place of the asthmatic 67bhp unit that the car came with; various other members provided the cash for tyres and entry fees.

It was agreed that Richard needed an experienced co-driver and he was paired with John King, an affable, unflappable dentist from Wokingham who had started rallying in what was then Southern Rhodesia. As King can reach for his wallet at a speed worthy of a gunslinger, it is near-impossible to buy him a drink and he characteristically paid most of the expenses when co-driving.

He was quite outstanding – he showed a natural talent immediately

They entered the Newtown Stages Rally in Mid Wales, completing it in 25th place and fourth in class. King was impressed, not just with his new driver's turn of speed, but his presence of mind. When he spun the car over a brow, he calmly did as he was told, driving against the rally route for a few yards to find somewhere wide enough to spin it round again. Plenty of novices would have hesitated or panicked.

'He was outstanding. He had natural talent and he had it immediately: it was talent that was there for all to see. That was the first thing. Secondly, he took every event very seriously. In other words, he was anxious to be fully prepared. I liked his approach, because so many drivers are doing it for the glory and then hope against hope that things will go right. Instead, with Richard, even from his very first rally, through his first formative years within rallying, he had a single-minded approach to it. There was nothing going to get in his way, in the nicest possible way,' King remembered.

Even with the motor club mucking in, it was a hand-to-mouth approach to an expensive pastime and funds were so tight that the Sunbeam was insured for its teenage driver only for the rallies themselves. Richard had no clear goal beyond wanting to contest the RAC Rally one day and he therefore concentrated on good-quality events run in forests, generally in Wales or northern England. It was a sensible, but financially draining policy. It meant that his overall results were less than startling, because he was contesting rallies that were invariably won by cars with four-wheel drive and infinitely more power, but he was soon winning his class and on Craven's 1988 rally on Bagshot's tank-testing tracks, he took the Sunbeam to fifth place overall.

The car did not last the year. The running costs were too great and it was sold to raise some cash (the engine was returned to Jarvis, naturally) and Richard resorted to borrowing a Corolla from Alec Cooper, another member of Craven, or Escorts from the likes of Churchill. The fact that he rarely damaged cars helped; indeed, he was well into his second season before he crashed a hired Escort in Radnor Forest on the Severn Valley Stages. Yet rallying is an almost entirely amateur sport and there was no material gain from helping an unknown, cash-strapped teenager. Richard's knack of bringing out the generosity in clubmen with cars of their own and, in some cases, businesses to run, provides absolute proof that professionalism is a veneer on sport's amateur core.

A 1989 rally at the Millbrook test track in Bedfordshire illustrated the point. It was a few weeks after Richard's first outright win, beating much more powerful machinery in Churchill's well-used Escort at Bagshot. Mike Chittenden had been at Bagshot then and, when a muddle with his co-driver prevented him from competing at Millbrook himself, he spotted Richard (who was meant to be servicing for Ewan) and offered him his Holbay-powered Escort for the day, on the spot. Once Richard had got the hang of a car with 50bhp more than he was used to and a borrowed crash helmet that tipped over his eyes, he won his class and finished on the edge of the top 10.

'Top bloke: not many people would do that,' Richard recalled. They keep in touch.

King navigated when available, but Richard used an even larger assortment of co-drivers than cars, the roll call including John Boother, Rodger Jenkins, Gavin Lawrence, Wayne Goble and Jan Churchill, among others.

To scrape money together, he turned his hand to everything from shelf-stacking in the Henley branch of Waitrose super-market to driving a baker's van, delivering cars for Reading Garage, packing mail order items and assembling Aeroquip brake hoses for Raceparts in Wallingford, as well as helping out at Churchill's rally school. The determination and the will-ingness to make sacrifices were not in doubt, yet Richard was fuelled by nothing more than the urge to rally as often as possible.

'It's strange. I still say it now, because it's still true. I never thought, "I want to be World Champion". Of course, you want to be a works driver, but I never thought, "This is what I'm doing it for". I never thought I was going to be World Champion. I just thought, "This is what I want to do and I'm reasonably good at it, and I want to win and I want to do it the best I can," but I never had it in my brain that this is what I was going to do for a career – and I never had it in my brain that I wanted to do anything else.

'I couldn't imagine – when ever any-body said, "What are you going to do?" I was like, "I don't know". I hadn't got a clue. I knew that I could live, because if the worst came to the worst, I could instruct and I could make a living, and it would be crap, but I knew that I could carry on, so I didn't have that worry. I was living with my parents, I didn't have any outgoings at all, so every penny I earned went on the rallying, but I never had the, "Right, it's 1990, by the end of this decade or by 1997 I want to be World Champion," or something like that. I never had that,' Richard insists.

His sister, who works for charities over-seas, once suggested that he ought to get a full-time job, but his parents never put

Like many budding rally drivers, Richard's career began in a 1,600cc Sunbeam, a £400 car that his father gave him for his 16th birthday. (Tony Large)

him under pressure. They had long since accepted that jobs had become a means to an end and that the end was rallying.

As Alex explained, 'He wasn't demanding. All he needed was his grub. He never went out boozing or dancing or cinema. You never minded, because he was so dedicated.'

Well after he began driving himself, Richard continued to seize any chance to watch rallies or even test sessions. One of his most vivid memories is of a five-day Toyota test at Churchill's rally school in preparation for the 1988 RAC.

'It was the year Kenneth [Eriksson] did the RAC with Toyota, and it blew up on the first stage. I was up there the whole week and I went up to the forest and for five days, I just stood watching them. Christ knows what I was doing. I remember Kenneth was driving for most of the test and I remember Juha [Kankkunen] coming and just doing the last day – so nothing changes there! I must have

February, 1988: Richard (foreground) poses with Gordon Jarvis, one of the guiding lights of his early career.

pestered everybody at Toyota so much and they must have felt sorry for me again. At the end of the test, right at the end, I sat in with Kenneth, going round the loop at Jan's and I was absolutely stunned. I was just gobsmacked. I would have been the most boring person in the world for the next month, telling everybody about it and I was so rooting for Kenneth, because I'd sat with him and then he bloody blew up on the first stage!'

Curiously, autotesting did as much for Richard's early career as rallying. Any number of people in Craven insist that he won the club's annual autotest, the Spinning Wheel, in his father's Cavalier. The fact that there is no record of his doing so (he was eighth in 1987 and fourth in 1988, winning his class on both occasions) and that it is a tiny event held purely for fun is beside the point. His ability to thread a Cavalier between cones as though it was a Mini made an indelible impression.

By the end of 1989, Richard's efforts at the wheel were merely preaching to the converted. Jarvis was convinced that the youngster was cut out for better things

than borrowing class-winning cars and suggested that he should contest the Peugeot GTI Challenge in 1990. No doubt an element of company loyalty was a factor, but it was undoubtedly the best chance of launching a professional career that British rally drivers had had since the Ford Escort Mexico championship of the early 1970s. Like the Mexicos, Peugeot's 1.6 and 1.9-litre 205GTIs were affordable cars that were quick enough to make a mark on national rallies and the manufacturer was prepared to provide publicity, training, prize money, cheap parts and, best of all, a works drive for the winner.

Craven's membership included fewer farmers than most motor clubs, but an otherwise typical cross-section of motor traders, mechanics, professionals and businessmen and one of these, a softly spoken, easy-going designer called David Williams (not related to the author), was not only an old friend of Jarvis's, but had already been prevailed upon to fund the occasional entry fee and a few tyres for Richard.

Williams, who is 16 years Richard's senior, cheerfully admits that he had treated work as a source of funding for a suc-

Running his own rally car was an expensive business and Richard proved quite adept at borrowing other people's cars, including Jan Churchill's RS2000 in May 1989. (Speedsports)

cession of rally cars since he came fourth on his first event in the early 1970s, driving an Anglia. He had rallied Escorts and Metro 6R4s with some success, and although he hadn't been much involved in Richard's progress to that point, he was a Burns fan. He had seen him in action on the Spinning Wheel and, as he said, 'I must admit that that was the turning point. I knew he was really, really good. Before that, he was a pestering kid with his dad, but after that, I knew he had something.'

It would be impossible to write this book without mentioning Williams and difficult to do so without making him sound like a mixture of saint and Svengali. But he was not impressed with the proposal that he should front up £32,000 for a season in the Peugeot. It was a substantial sum and he suggested that Richard should try harder to raise some sponsorship of his own. It was a dispiriting prospect. Alex and Denise had written hundreds of letters to no avail. Richard and Jarvis decided that there was no sense in dwelling on 1990 until the RAC was out of the way.

Williams was licking his wounds after ploughing a good deal of money to little purpose into a works-type Lancia Delta and therefore decided to make a day of watching the RAC Rally stage at Silverstone rather than participating. The Peugeot Challenge runners made an immediate impression.

'They were extraordinarily average, and I was looking at it and going, "I could do that. Maybe I should do the Peugeot Challenge",' he remembered. 'Then I said, "I know who would be much better at this: Richard." I just said to myself, "When I get home, I want to 'phone Richard up and tell him he's going to do

Jan Churchill played a large part in Richard's early development, providing work, encouragement and guidance.

the Peugeot Challenge". And I went home and told him he was going to do it. I thought it through and now I was running my own business, I had an idea of how to do things.'

At a meeting at the Burns's house, he explained his plan to the family, to Jarvis and Mick Shonfield, who had worked at Reading Garage and now ran his own garage in Reading, Autocare. There was prize money of £1,000 per rally for winning, with more at the end of the year. If Richard made a steady start – he would have to learn about the 205, after all – did not crash too often, and improved steadily, prize money could cover running costs. If Jarvis arranged hire purchase, a few of them chipped in to put a deposit down on a second-hand 205GTI and did not mind having money tied up until the car was sold at the end of the season, the total cost would be more like £4,000 or £5,000. Within minutes, a pile of cheques amounting to over £2,000 was on the dining room table.

'It was like all my Christmases had come at once,' Richard said.

'All it was, was a matter of cash flow,' Williams explained. In fact, he paid in a little more to cover the initial cost of the car. For that first season, there was no sponsorship as such other than £600 from Reading Garage, although the Peugeot naturally bore allegiance to Autocare and Williams's firm at the time, Innervisions. Why should anyone have wanted to sponsor an unknown rally driver from Reading?

Within a few weeks, a second-hand 205GTI had been bought and Shonfield took charge of converting it into a rally car. Williams had proposed a few rules. The first was that no-one would be paid. The second was that there would be nothing amateur about the team's appearance. Quite apart from his design background, Jarvis had taught him that there is no reason why rally cars should be anything other than immaculate and it could only

improve their chances of getting sponsorship. Each member of the team bought his own Peugeot rally jacket, at a cost of £50 each.

Richard has since become a competent mechanic – World Championship servicing restrictions practically demand it – but at that stage, his role in car preparation was confined to cutting out mudguards with a Stanley knife, a process that usually led to sliced fingers, and making sure that the car was smart. If he wanted to be a works driver, he was told that in the meantime, he would have to repaint sills and jerry cans, scrape the mud off wheels, keep the car and the service van clean and polished, and carry out the simpler, often tedious aspects of maintenance. The team had regular meetings to review progress and discuss forthcoming events, and there was always a long list of jobs for the driver.

Neat as ever, Richard flicks Alec Cooper's Corolla around a Welsh hairpin.

Shonfield good naturedly suggested that Richard did not always take quite as much care of his own appearance as the car's.

'He never even had a wardrobe. He had boxfuls of sweatshirts and jackets that people had given him. We used to turn up all smart, trying to look like a works team and he'd turn up with these jeans with the knees sticking out.'

Once the car was finished, it was taken to Churchill's rally school for its first test. Just possibly, it was a little too smart and, for the first and last time, Williams passed comment on Richard's driving.

'Richard was driving it like a hairdresser, so I drove this thing and I drove it backwards and forwards, getting faster and faster and faster, and more and more sideways, until I got to the point where the car was completely sideways and I touched the corner of it, and it flipped and it went straight over. Richard had never been in a car that had flipped before. I was down there and he was up there, and I told him not to press the seatbelt, because I didn't want this lanky lump landing on me.

If you want to roll it, just go and find out what the limit is in it

'It knocked all the windows out, smashed it to smithereens, our beautiful car. Richard and I got out, pushed it on its wheels and it did start up, and I drove this pile of wreckage without the front windscreen back to the boys, who'd basically given the last two or three months of their lives to building this. It was terrible, the stick I got.

'Alex and Gordon and some other people were coming up to see the car the next day, and they all met us in the pub. We didn't have mobile 'phones in those days, and we kept on talking to them about apple turnovers and upside down cake, and we didn't tell them. We couldn't! Of course, we all thought it was really funny, because we were all drunk, and then we actually told them that I'd rolled it. You've never seen anything like their faces, it was

just a picture. And I lost my confidence a lot after that, because I felt like a right prat, which I was.

'We thought the best thing we could do was get the car repaired and let Richard drive absolutely flat out for one day, with a temporary windscreen – every panel bashed to smithereens. We checked it all out and I think this is where Richard's speed came from, because like many things in the Richard Burns-David Williams story, lots of it involves luck. Richard spent the whole of the next day driving this car, totally unafraid of bending it, driving it at the most incredible angles, learning what to do with a Peugeot rally car. If it had been all pristine, like it was, he would have driven it all nice and neatly. We said, "If you want to roll it again, just go and find out what the limit is. That's it, Richard. Do whatever you want to do. Chuck it into the boulders, chuck it against the tree if you want! I personally will pay for all this. I will sort the whole thing out. You just do what you want to do."

'If that hadn't happened, Richard would have been really nervous about driving the car on the first stage, so I think that was a major point in Richard's career. He'd learnt the limit of the car. He'd learnt all sorts of things in that one day.'

When the 1990 Peugeot Challenge runners gathered in Llandrindrod Wells in Mid Wales for the Panaround Rally, the nerves were banished. Against a record field of 48 Peugeots, Burns and his new co-driver, Jason Murphy (a friend from his Under 17s CC days) were fastest on the first stage and romped to a handsome victory, despite a spin on the sixth stage.

Looking at the results, it is tempting to assume that Burns simply brushed the Peugeot opposition aside and that talented drivers such as Ricky Evans and Clive Wheeler were made to look second rate. That wasn't the case. Ten years on, asked if he has ever encountered a driver he believed might be better than he was, Burns immediately singled out both Wheeler and Julian Reynolds. Besides, his first Peugeot campaign nearly ran into

serious trouble on the second event, his own club's Imber Rally, which was held on asphalt military roads on the western side of Salisbury Plain.

Richard scored a narrow victory on the road in spite of a query over a road penalty between stages, but was thrown out afterwards. Peugeot Challenge rules were strict and thorough post-event scrutineering to make sure that cars were legal was very much part of it. Richard turned up three minutes past the appointed time and was therefore excluded. Keith Baud, the championship co-ordinator, would have been within his rights in docking all his points, but he made a dispensation and deprived him of the Imber tally alone. Richard took it on the chin.

That was the last major setback. In fact, it was the last time that he was beaten on a Peugeot Challenge rally. There were times in 1990 when Reynolds led him or Evans set more fastest stage times but, as Baud put it, 'He's so bloody consistent, isn't he? Consistent and fast.'

Within months, rumours were spreading like wildfire, that Burns had a separate car for Tarmac rallies and that he was

The Holbay-powered Escort was the most powerful car Richard had rallied at the time – and he wasn't even planning to compete when he arrived at the start of the rally. He adapted swiftly enough.

being bankrolled by Williams, a multi-millionaire businessman. It wasn't so. In fact, funds were so meagre in the first year that Richard made do with a standard engine rather than the painstakingly tuned Skip Brown units preferred by the best of his rivals and the team always stayed in bed and breakfasts rather than hotels, but the Autocare squad did provide some material for the rumour mongers.

At one race in that year's series, at Donington, for example, Williams managed to borrow some tyre warmers and arranged for a friend to turn up with a Ferrari. 'Hot stuff' it said above the number plate. As it happened, the tyre warmers were not plugged in and the Peugeot's standard engine ensured that Richard ended up fifth, but the ploy had a certain psychological value.

Baud was a scrupulously independent observer and dismisses any suggestion that money had anything to do with

Richard's success, any more than it had aided the first Peugeot Challenge winner, Paul Frankland.

'They just went about it in a very professional way ... I don't think people realised that because we were so hard on the competitors if they cheated and were so strong on the car preparation and trying to make the cars as equal as possible, it didn't matter how much money you had. If you couldn't drive the bloody thing, you couldn't drive it. Richard was very much like Paul Frankland the first year. Paul never had a lot of money, but he was a very smooth driver, which is what you needed to be in those cars and Paul never scratched a car. Richard was just the same. He never used to put a mark on that car and that must make his rallying cheaper to start with, if he's not having to rebuild the car all the while.'

He's one of a handful of youngsters to rally a factory car

Owing to its popularity, Peugeot had divided the challenge in two that year and the two classes did not meet until the British Open Championship Audi Sport Rally in Wales that October. Richard, who had been contesting the junior division, was fresh from another Peugeot win on his first international rally, the Tour of Flanders, and promptly beat allcomers to take 16th overall.

'Burns is the best,' proclaimed *Motoring News* and yet Richard admitted that he had driven with something in hand, as he needed the car the following weekend for the Zuiderzee Rally in the Netherlands. The idea was to team up once again with his Flanders navigator, Jerry Freeman, and learn more about pace notes. They duly finished third in class against much more powerful 16-valve Astras.

Freeman, whose brother Roger won the British Open Championship co-driving Mark Lovell, is a Pirelli technician who has since accompanied near-enough every rally driver worth the name in testing and, like almost everyone with first-hand experience of co-driving Richard,

he was bowled over by the experience.

'His car control, I tell you, the only other one in my memory who had the same amount of natural car control was Mark Lovell. There's an immense difference between Lovell and Richard, but in the way they drove, very similar. They were just really calm and cool, and never got that excited. It was such an enjoyable place to be, sitting next to him.

'Zuiderzee Rally, along a straight there was a chicane – or it wasn't quite a chicane, but it was like a gate and it wasn't quite straight. And when we were practising, he just got out at this gate and had a look and carried on going. And then I realised what he was doing when we came up to it flat out and I was thinking, "Good God, he's not slowing down!"

'And he said after, "I sussed it, that the Peugeot would just fit through there, even by just unbalancing it". I thought, "For God's sake!" As we went through it, he was changing up. You wouldn't have got anybody else doing that. He was so smooth, so precise, so tidy.'

Up to a point, anyway: 'We had moments in there, with that little Peugeot. Bumping along the top of the dyke, we hit this bump that neither of us had seen in the recce and we flew along the floor, nose-down, and I was waiting for it to go end over end, but it didn't. Oh my life. I think that was probably the closest I've ever come to an immense accident and never had it. Somebody was holding on to the rear bumper as we flew. Those two things I'll never forget about Zuiderzee Rally.'

Within three years of driving in his first rally, Richard was not simply contesting the RAC Rally, but doing so in a works car, a Group N Peugeot 309GTI. He remains one of a handful of teenagers to have rallied a factory car. Naturally, the press had begun to take an interest.

'I didn't expect to do this well at the start of the year. I got to the end of the first stage of the Panaround and someone said, "You're 20 seconds ahead of the nearest Peugeot". I was aghast. When I started the Challenge, the RAC drive was just too far ahead to think about … I don't think there's going to be any pressure on me apart from the fact that I've got to prove that this year has been no fluke,' he told *Motoring News*.

The RAC was much the longest and hardest rally he had contested, and the first time he had competed in a forest at night. He was teamed with one of Williams's former co-drivers, Wayne Goble, and more than justified Peugeot's faith in him by finishing 28th and seventh in class, despite a puncture and problems with the gear linkage after hitting a rock.

The Craven crowd reckoned that their job was done. Richard had exceeded their wildest expectations, the prize money had balanced the books and now, inevitably, their hyper-talented teenager would be snapped up by a far-sighted works team. It had been tremendous fun, but all good things come to an end. They would sell the car and reclaim their deposits.

But the telephone never rang. Des O'Dell, Peugeot's competitions supremo in Britain, indicated that he thought Richard needed a little more experience. There was nothing for it but to take the risky option of returning to a championship Richard had conquered already. There was no money for anything else. Richard agrees that his career would have foundered without such unstinting support, yet he was neither daunted nor embarrassed.

'I never thought of it like that. I was just so grateful that they were helping. I'm sure at the time I didn't even seem that grateful. They wanted to do it, because at the time they could see what I wasn't even really thinking of, I suppose. They could see that I was so into it that I wasn't going to take no for an answer from anybody, plus they were all people who were already involved in rallying anyway and enjoying it, so they saw it as a good outlet for them. It virtually stopped all their other rallying activities. I certainly don't think I could have made it without them, no. I could have maybe gone the wrong way with people who maybe didn't have quite such a good view of the future.'

'When you think about it, I suppose he was spoilt. We all spoiled him, but we all enjoyed doing what we did,' Shonfield reflected. He concedes that the occasional spanner went flying when he was beneath the car, but there was never a harsh word between the members of the team.

The Audi Sport had provided more than a resounding class win. As Murphy had work commitments and an impending marriage to consider, the Craven team had been seeking a new co-driver. Afterwards, Richard had got into conversation with Robert Reid, who was co-driving his nearest rival on that occasion, Steve Egglestone, and the two met again during the recce for the RAC. As a result, Reid travelled south to meet the Burns selection committee in readiness for 1991.

He was four years older and had more experience than his driver, having co-driven the likes of Robbie Head and Stephen Price after making a name for himself on navigational rallies. Indeed, he had even contested and won the Hackle Rally with Colin McRae earlier that year, when the future World Champion had dumbfounded the Scottish Championship contenders by beating them in his uncle's battle-weary RS2000.

There were obvious differences in age and background (Reid comes from a prosperous potato-farming family in Perthshire) but he was every bit as dedicated as Burns, highly ambitious and utterly meticulous. He was recruited without hesitation. It is hard to identify the precise factor that makes a partnership between driver and co-driver work; in theory, any of the top drivers should perform equally well with any of the top co-drivers, leaving aside any language barrier. The reality is somewhat different. Burns and Reid struck up an instant rapport and there is a widespread belief that Reid has been indispensable ever since. Baud noticed it at once.

'I'm not for one moment suggesting

I was so into it I wouldn't take no as an answer from anyone

that Richard hadn't got the ability, but it was noticeable in that second year of the Challenge, once Robert was in the left-hand seat, Richard was just totally unbeatable. Nobody could even get a look at him. I'm not saying his own abilities hadn't improved at that time, but Robert made that little bit of extra difference, just gelled it all for him, I think.'

The team noticed the difference, too. Shonfield remembers turning up in Dinant for the Circuit des Ardennes that year and discovering that Reid's instructions made life as straightforward as if he had been driving from Reading to Newbury.

Richard's father liked Robert, but had slightly mixed feelings nonetheless: 'At one time, I seriously thought about installing another telephone. It got beyond a joke. It was that bad. We had more rows about that than anything, the amount of time he spent on the bloody 'phone. You literally couldn't get on the 'phone.'

Williams had managed to find a sponsor, the computer company, Elonex, which contributed £2,500. That would not get a sticker on the rear bumper of Burns's Subaru now, but it represented a useful sum then and it was one of the factors that contributed to a Skip Brown engine for 1991. It was indicative of the goodwill between Peugeot Challenge competitors that Richard was also sponsored by Tamworth Windscreens, the company run by one of his main rivals, Ricky Evans.

The prize money was soon gushing in. Richard walked away with a class win on the Wyedean after Reynolds hit clutch trouble and he dominated again on the Circuit des Ardennes, which he still recalls as one of his most satisfying rallies. Demanding stages that jinked their way through villages and the fact that Belgian recces were then conducted at a speed

Richard was an overnight success in the Peugeot GTI Challenge and a consistent winner in Britain's most competitive junior rally championship in years. (Tony Large)

32

that made them a spectator sport in their own right made for an unforgettable experience – even if the practice car was a very tired Fiat Uno.

By the end of March, he had earned £800 in prize money and amassed twice as many points as his rival. 'For Peugeot Challenge Reid Burns' quipped *Motoring News*. The team decided to skip the next round, the Tour of Lincolnshire, which is not renowned for classic stages, in favour of contesting the Welsh International.

It was the right move. Richard finished 13th overall against far more potent machinery, then clinched the 1991 Challenge as early as the first week of July, by finishing in a remarkable seventh place on the Kayel Graphics Rally, a round of Britain's main national championship in Glamorgan.

The well-worn claim that Group N cars such as the Burns 205GTI were in 'show-

Des O'Dell, Peugeot's competitions chief in Britain, took a close personal interest in the GTI Challenge and, inevitably, in the progress of its teenage star. Richard was not only quick, but conscientious. He never missed the optional training days.

room' specification is a touch misleading. Microchip tuning of the engine management system alone could make a noticeable difference, to say nothing of better dampers or brake material. Nevertheless, the engine and gearbox were essentially standard and there would have been plenty of competitors who had driven to the rally in quicker machinery. Richard's results were nothing short of breathtaking.

It had not been quite as straightforward as it may have appeared. In February, when snow was forecast for the Talkland Rally, the first round of the 1991 British Open Championship, Williams suggested that Richard might like to take over the entry. Richard seized the opportunity and galloped into a seven-minute class lead in the North Yorkshire forests before the gearbox failed.

There was just about time to rebuild it for the following weekend's Challenge round, the Panaround, but when Shonfield dismantled it he found that the gearbox casing was full of melted scrap.

Later that day, Richard returned from Peugeot's competitions department in

Coventry with a grin as wide as the River Thames. O'Dell had given him a brand-new gearbox. It was another testament to Richard's persuasiveness and a hint that O'Dell had overcome some of his earlier misgivings about the Challenge's hottest property.

The new gearbox did not quite avert the crisis. It turned out that the flywheel was scrap as well – but that was not discovered until the night before the start. Williams and Gavin Lawrence drove back to Reading to get a new one and the car was eventually in combat trim shortly before daybreak. Once it was running, the van was badly damaged when an errant rally car ran into the front of it and the Autocare crew relied on other competitors to help them reach the next service point. Richard's progress to another class win was far less dramatic.

By then, Peugeot had started taking a serious interest. Richard was loaned a works 309 for both the Mid Wales Stages (when Chris Wood temporarily replaced Reid) and the Scottish. On the Manx International in September, he demolished the opposition at night to take a convincing class win with the same car, having lost ground earlier with two punctures. Back in his own Peugeot, he bagged another class victory on the Audi Sport, thereby taking the 2-litre Group N prize in the British Open Championship.

A Burns bandwagon was gathering speed. He was still gaining experience at every opportunity, watching rallies he couldn't contest, always eager to help and learn. Meanwhile, Williams had made approaches to Prodrive, the Banbury concern that ran Subaru's works team.

As a result, Richard got his first taste of four-wheel drive in August 1991, finishing third on the Border Rally in southern Scotland in a Prodrive Legacy. He did not win the Group N production class, though. That went to Dom Buckley Junior, who was second in a Mazda.

Buckley was a rival. Keenly aware that there was an unprecedented crop of

The Autocare crew (clockwise from front left): Mick Shonfield, Gordon Jarvis, Richard Burns, David Williams, Alex Burns and Gavin Lawrence, pose with the 205 and some of Richard's trophies.

young British rally talent, Shell announced a scheme it had already employed to good effect in motorcycle racing. The Shell Scholarship would be awarded to the year's most promising young rally driver, who would be provided with a fully paid drive in a Group N Sierra Cosworth 4x4 in 1992.

Burns was inevitably a candidate. The field was slimmed down to six, the other five being Buckley, Robbie Head, Mark Higgins, Jonny Milner and Alister McRae, Colin's younger brother. All of them were under 25 and they all proved more than capable of earning a living as professional drivers. There was not a makeweight among them.

Peugeot had a link with Shell and had no doubt that Richard was the ideal candidate. Baud commended him to the selection committee.

'It has been interesting seeing him grow in 18 months from a young man still unsure of himself and his own abilities into a thoroughly professional and competent driver,' he wrote at the time.

Looking back on Richard's Peugeot apprenticeship, he commented, 'Basically, he was as perfect as you could ever want: he drove well, he was presentable, he never barked the cars. It was almost as though people were suspicious. Is there something in the British psyche that doesn't like perfection and has to knock people like that down?'

The Craven crew were counting on Shell. There was nothing else on offer beyond the Peugeot prize drive on the RAC, when Richard took a considerably more powerful Group A 309 to 16th place and a class win, although he was beaten by the more experienced and highly gifted Dave Metcalfe, driving a 1,600cc works Nova. However, Richard had not tested the 309 on a dirt road before the start and he held off Milner, who had a good deal

Richard's domination of his second season in the Peugeot Challenge allowed him to contest an increasing range of non-Challenge rallies, including the 1991 Welsh. It yielded a convincing class win. (Gavin Lodge)

more experience of his 205, albeit less power.

When interviewed, Richard's innate caution stood out as conspicuously as his driving ability. He said that he wanted 'to go a lot further than any British driver has been. If you look at my record, I haven't had any stunning results, whereas a lot of the others have.'

Everything possible was done to prepare him for the Shell examination, which would include a drive on a loose-surface special stage at Silverstone, a drive around the track and interviews for driver and co-driver.

Interviews had been part of Richard's training for a while. Jarvis had taken a home video camera to Challenge rounds and, while Richard had shied away from it at first, he had become a more fluent speaker as the months passed. As Gordon said, Richard had better get used to the idea that he would be interviewed by Tony Mason for the BBC one day. The team devised a mock interview at home in the days before the Scholarship assessment in mid-November.

The day of reckoning showed promise. Higgins's karting background was one of the factors that made him the most impressive performer on the circuit, but the rally judges – the respected Ulster driver, Bertie Fisher, and the double British Open Champion, David Llewellin – were agreed that Burns was the pick of the bunch on the stage.

'His car control – the thing stood out, you know? It was all so natural. He wasn't having to try to impress, if you like. He was just cool and level. At the end of the day, he would have been our choice from a driving point of view,' Fisher confirmed. Llewellin was just as impressed, not just by the Burns technique, but at the way he adapted it to very different cars.

The committee was divided, but after a prolonged debate, reputedly curtailed only because television wanted a decision before nightfall, it was announced that the winner was Alister McRae. There was no denying that the standard was exceptionally high, but none either that the news was greeted with astonishment – 'Shell shock' – as *Motoring News* put it the following week. Alister himself could scarcely believe it, thinking that his Nova's unreliability in 1991 (Burns had beaten him on the Welsh) and his name would tell against him.

Since then, both Burns and McRae have become World Championship drivers and the Shell Scholarship is a matter of historical record, but at the time it caused immense controversy and, much as the two drivers might seek to deny it, some bitterness. A decade later, committee members remain evasive.

It had been agreed that everyone would stay the night after, win or lose. In the car on his way back to the hotel, Richard was in tears. It was his first serious reverse and a damning reverse at that, one that left him stranded with no car and no money in the middle of a recession: Shell's judges had made it plain that in their view, he was second best.

Williams was livid. Libel laws make his views on the episode unprintable. 'Richard and Robert were staying in a hotel down the road from Silverstone and I must admit I cried all the way back, not with displeasure, but with anger at the whole thing. I had some rock music turned up, I was like, "I will beat those fuckers!" – like that. I went up to Richard's and Robert's bedroom and I said, "I don't care how much it costs, what I need to do, whatever it's going to take. You two will be doing the British Championship next year. I don't care what it takes." And I meant it.'

British men are not encouraged to betray anything that might be regarded as emotional weakness. But crying can be a constructive thing.

I don't care what it takes, you will be doing the next Championship

chapter three

And the championships keep coming

There was no budget and no programme, but there was a car, as the wounds left by the Delta had healed and Williams had returned to competition himself the year before, in a Group N Sierra Cosworth 4x4. However, Prodrive was keen to get privateers into Subarus and, after testing a Group N Legacy with Colin McRae at Bruntingthorpe, Williams bought one with a view to contesting the 1992 Mintex national championship. If only he could raise the budget, he decided, Richard could drive the same car in the British international series and give Alister McRae and Shell a run for their money.

I went out and asked everyone I knew for money

'I asked Elonex, which was a young company at the time, for sponsorship, as they had sponsored us before. I asked them for a lot more money this year – I think about £25–30,000 – and I asked a number of other companies for money. I forced myself to go out and do it. I went out and asked everybody I knew for money for it. I asked Subaru and I asked everybody.

'And surprisingly, I asked Shell. There was some sort of deal between Shell and Subaru in the UK, which I didn't know about, but they had some money which

was for anyone running a Subaru and I didn't go after it, it just fell in my lap, so long as it was called the Shell Team Subaru. So I ended up with a load of money from Elonex, a load of money from Shell and a load of money from all the various smaller companies, such as Response Computer Maintenance.

'We didn't run it with Gordon and Alex and those guys, because they were really experienced in Peugeots. We used a bloke called Ron Hill, who used to be my own co-driver and a lot of his friends who used to be my mechanics when I ran my Sierra Cosworth and my Nissan. So I took it away from Richard's house and put it in Ron's garage, which was next to his house, and we ran Shell Team Subaru out of this really small garage. Without anyone making a profit out of it and no one being paid, all that money became a huge budget to actually run the car.'

It was an enticing prospect. The Legacy shared very little with the ungainly 1980s Subarus that had appealed to the practical rather than the fashionable. Like the Sierra, it had a 2-litre turbocharged engine and in certain respects, notably suspension, it was potentially a better car. Richard would not only get a chance to prove his worth, but to gain overall results far beyond the Peugeot's capabilities.

As it turned out, the first casualty was the plan. The economics of running rallies on Forestry Commission land were bleeding organisers white: as costs rose and entries declined, they needed to raise entry fees to avoid crippling losses in case they did not get the maximum number of competitors, then found that the break-even fee was so high that it deterred all but the wealthiest and most determined crews, which meant that entries plunged yet further, forcing them to cancel rallies after all. Yorkshire's first round of the British Championship was one of the main victims, much to Richard's disappointment. Williams agreed to forego the first Mintex round, the Bournemouth-based Mazda Winter Rally, so that his 'team-mate' could have a run instead.

Richard responded with one of the drives that made his reputation. There was no shortage of four-wheel-drive opposition, much of it with more power and plenty of other modifications not allowed in Group N; Trevor Smith, one of Britain's most able national drivers, was a comfortable winner in his Sierra Cosworth.

Entering the last stage, Wytch Farm, Richard was third, 12 seconds down on Bill Barton's Metro 6R4 – a little too far behind to stand any real chance of depriving a capable opponent of second with only 5.5 stage miles to go. That was the theory anyway.

January weather made a mockery of the arithmetic. It was dark, wet and foggy and, to Barton's incredulity, Burns sliced through the murk as though guided by a laser to gain 27 seconds and second place. It was a quite sensational performance – a jaw-dropping display of skill and hunger – that had involved driving at over 75mph when he could scarcely see the end of the bonnet. As Smith was not registered for the Mintex series, Richard had gained maximum points and Williams realised that he had probably seen the last of his car for the season.

In truth, that result flattered the Legacy. In most circumstances, the Group N version was no real match for a

Cosworth. Transmission problems led to retirement on the first round of the British Open series that ran, the Vauxhall Sport Rally in North Wales, while Richard made do with a lowly 41st on the next round, the Pirelli International, after drowning out in a ford in Kielder Forest and picking up a couple of punctures. Three more punctures a week later, on the next Mintex qualifier, the Granite City Rally, meant that he was no better than eighth at the finish in Aberdeen. The Group N winner on each occasion? Alister McRae, who won the Granite City outright and took an impressive third overall

Caps, like cars, seemed to fit. Even though he was competing against much more potent opposition, in 1992 Richard maintained his record of winning a championship a year. (Gavin Lodge)

on the Pirelli. He had won the Lakeland Rally for good measure. Far from slugging it out toe to toe, Richard was struggling to lay a glove on the Shell Scholar.

Easter brought better news, as he was third in Churchill's 911 on his return to Imber, beaten only by four-wheel-drive cars. Indeed, he would have been second if he hadn't completed some of the stages under the target time.

It was a fleeting respite. On the Manx National, the Legacy was in one of its sulkier moods and Richard lost time with gearbox and turbo trouble, then burst over a brow to find Pete Doughty's Sierra stranded with electrical failure on one of the narrowest parts of the route. There was not the slightest chance of avoiding the impact but the one consolation was that Ron Hill had almost a month to resurrect the remains in time for the Scottish event. Richard was in some need of a good result. He clearly was not going to salvage much from the Open Championship and needed to make his Mintex performances tell.

In the early stages on the Scottish, he traded times with the father of the McRae clan, Jim, and when the Subaru behaved, he could just about match Alister, but then the engine began to misfire and he limped home in 10th. It was all good experience, but not quite the stuff of which headlines are made.

On the Severn Valley, his luck turned at last. He was in the running for victory all day and finally held off Murray Grierson to score his biggest win thus far and regain the Mintex championship lead. A well-deserved victory restored some momentum to a character-building campaign, but luck had certainly played its part. The gearbox reported sick just before the final stage at the Royal Welsh Showground in Builth Wells and it seized on the finish ramp; it was just as well that the start and finish had not been in the same place, a few miles up the road in Llandrindod Wells.

Richard carefully negotiates a sodden Kielder track during the 1992 Pirelli Rally. The Group N Legacy was not at its best in water. (Gavin Lodge)

There were two rounds to go, the Kayel Graphics in South Wales and the *Rally Car* stages in Yorkshire. Richard and Robert were not to be denied now, finishing second in Glamorgan even though the Legacy tended to misfire when hot, then clinching the title with third place in Yorkshire.

'There is definitely a knack to winning and this pair seem to have it. Winning this championship has been about consistency and stepping up a gear when the opportunities to grab extra points have come along. Once again, Richard has given the impression that there is plenty left to come,' *Motoring News* commented.

As usual, Richard had done everything asked of him and in the process, he had perhaps made winning the national title look easier than it was.

'It had no power at all and – it was not

Winning rallies in the Legacy was hard work but the months of endeavour were rewarded with a conclusive victory on the Kerridge Rally in Mid Wales. (Gavin Lodge)

a dodgy car – but the suspension we had changed every other rally from White Power [dampers], to Bilstein to something else and none of it had ever been really set up properly, and you go through a ford on the Pirelli Rally and it goes on to one cylinder. We never did any testing in it at all – nothing – so for the Manx, it was like, "Well, the suspension should be OK," and the wheels would break. It was run a little bit on a wing most of the time. We did the best we could,' was Richard's verdict.

Aside from driving ability, Richard's success was owed to thought and preparation rather than money. Guided principally by Williams, he was encouraged to consider every detail that might make him a better driver – and his approach had not gone unnoticed at Prodrive. Midway through the season, Richard was given the first of a small number of tests in a full works, Group A Legacy.

In his formative years, Colin McRae had visited a few World Championship rounds, driving a service vehicle, helping out and getting the lie of the land.

In Group N form, the Legacy was outgunned by most of its opposition in 1992. Richard's flair and commitment regularly masked its failings. (Gavin Lodge)

Williams suggested that Richard should follow suit and he jumped at the chance; there was never a hint of pride – no suggestion that as a national championship leader, he might be above sleeping in a van or on someone's floor.

As he discovered on the Acropolis, life is somewhat different outside the Home Counties. He had already been fined for speeding – quite an achievement in itself, given the legendary tolerance the Greek police display towards any sort of traffic infringement during the rally – and then he unwittingly reversed into a beggar crouched in a gutter. He was promptly thrown into a police cell for several hours. Naturally, he got no sympathy when he was released. Instead, the mechanics bound him hand and foot with tie wraps, made a template and sprayed him with black, prison-uniform arrows.

Williams was proud of the fact that his pupil was never too proud, but well aware that there was a streak of laziness too – as Richard would be the first to acknowledge – and that the willowy youth needed to work constantly on his fitness. Stamina

had been a problem even in the Peugeot Challenge, on relatively short, cool rallies in a car that was none too physical to drive. Williams had therefore introduced Richard to Liz Linford.

'She came on board, even earlier, in the Peugeot days – she joined him for free as well – telling him what to do. Richard and Liz got on extremely well, and Richard started training and believing in eating the right things, right from an early age. Remember, no one else was doing that in those days. Richard would have aromatherapy and he would have reflexology and have body massages, and was eating bananas and cornflakes while everyone else was eating meat pies and drinking beer. He was well ahead of the game with that. We got him colour-analysed, we got people in to help him with his talking and communications skills. After every event, we used to sit down and look for 10 things to improve – on every event. And it would be another 10 things and another 10 things, and it would be to do with the weight of the co-driver, the weight of the driver, the stamina, the thickness of the notepaper – every single little bit of detail we would go into, every single thing, no matter how minute. After 10 rallies, we'd done 100 improvements.'

There was always something new to try or to learn. Richard contested a round of the Escort RS2000 championship, finishing second in class to Tony Dron at the Loton Park hillclimb and he also joined the *Top Gear* team for a kart race at Le Mans. On certain rallies, he was part of the gravel note crew, checking road conditions and amending pace notes where necessary for the likes of Colin McRae and Ari Vatanen.

Prodrive was certainly interested – impressed, even – but it was in no hurry to

offer the 21-year-old a works contract. Williams would need to be a little more persuasive than that.

'We thought, "Well, there's only one way to do this. We're actually going to get the money to do this." So I went off and asked Elonex again for 10 times the budget we had before and I asked a number of clients, and we had driver's days and all sorts of things to try to raise money, and it scared the living daylights out of me doing this, because it's not really what I do,' Williams confessed.

There were alternatives, chiefly with Ford teams. Williams approached the factory team at Boreham, and Malcolm Wilson, who was then in the process of starting M-Sport, but eventually turned to Steve Black, who was also linked with Peugeot and was running the Shell Scholarship Sierra.

In the end, the budget needed to run a works-specification Subaru to an appropriate standard was simply out of reach. Williams decided that it would be best to agree terms with Black's firm, SBG, to run an Escort Cosworth in the British

As his experience increased, so did the power of the cars that came his way. Richard borrowed Jan Churchill's Porsche 911 for the 1992 Imber Rally, finishing a close third. (Tony Large)

Championship and informed Prodrive that regrettably he could not raise the cash. At that point, Prodrive's Managing Director, David Richards, told him that the deal was on. He would take the Elonex money. Prodrive would find or fund the difference for a British Championship campaign in 1993.

Williams was bold enough to ask for a little more: he wanted Richard to drive for the factory, rather than the customer team. Prodrive consented and the deal was made public at the end of October. Richard was not a works driver exactly, but his ascent to stardom looked irresistible, his talent rewarded. The hard work and the horse trading were very much behind the scenes.

For Williams, who was more used to working in exhibition design, these were treacherous, shark-infested waters. A fortnight after doing a deal with the Mintex Champion, Prodrive announced that it would be defending Colin McRae's back-to-back British titles with a two-car 'junior team'. Richard was to be joined in a works Group A Legacy in 1993 by Alister McRae. Jim had promised to bring a sponsor of his own.

There were well-established links between Prodrive and Lanark's rallying dynasty. Quite apart from Colin's electrifying successes and Jim's own past with the team (he had driven its Metro 6R4 to great effect in 1986), Alister had sampled the Group N Legacy too, driving it on the 1991 RAC. Besides, Richard had not beaten him all season and Alister had not only walked away with Group N in the British Open Championship, but finished third

Putting a brave face on his first trip to the Acropolis, Richard poses with an Isuzu Trooper sign-written like a fighter plane – but totting up fines and trips to gaol rather than enemies shot down.

overall, more than justifying Shell's faith.

'It's sowing seed corn,' Richards stated, revealing that both the youngsters would have two-year options. To the stunned Burns camp, it looked more like sowing dissension in the ranks.

It is an old saying that your most dangerous opponent is your team-mate, and never more so than when that team-mate is also young and gifted, and has something to prove. The tension was undeniable, especially as the McRae sponsor, whoever it was, turned out to be a very shy company that did not want its name on the car. Both Legacys ran in Elonex colours throughout 1993 and money became increasingly tight. Richard concedes that the atmosphere was not exactly soothing.

'I was a bit pissed off at the start of it,

Versatility is one of the rally driver's key attributes. After a year spent in a four-wheel-drive Subaru, Richard reverted to front-wheel drive and Peugeot in the autumn. (Gavin Lodge)

because it was like every step I take, it was "wham"! The McRaes would put a wall in front of me or something. All they were doing was trying to get the best thing possible for Alister. I don't think it was ever bad to be honest, because it wasn't like they were doing anything evil or nasty – which you knew at the time as well.'

He subsequently discovered that a good deal more was riding on his success than even he imagined. Williams had got Elonex to do the deal by underwriting it himself. If Richard didn't win the title, he promised, Elonex would not have to pay a penny.

With the Mintex title secured, Richard went back to Peugeot in the autumn, driving a Group A 309 on both the Elonex Rally (a new name for the Audi Sport) and the RAC. He finished outside the top 10 on the former, having lost seven minutes with ignition problems, although he gained a class win even so. On the RAC, he was very creditably keeping Metcalfe in sight until the 309's wheel studs sheared

and he retired in Kielder, leaving the class win to the Kendal man's 2-litre Astra.

Conscientious to a fault, Richard knew that he had to make the most of his new-found eminence. He agreed to contribute a column to *Motoring News* and organised his own pre-season press conference, at TGI Friday's in Reading. It was the right idea, but a touch naïve. He did not appreciate that while it might be his sort of place, Fleet Street generally needs a Michelin star or two if it's going to be lured outside London to meet a little-known sportsman and a slim audience therefore consisted of the usual suspects and a man from the local newspaper.

Most sportsmen's columns are ghost-written and, while Richard's was no exception, he showed a good deal more interest than most in seeing the finished article before it went to press. It was much more unusual, but equally in character, that he also wanted a say in the choice of photographs; he has a streak of vanity.

Richard made a favourable impression

on Prodrive management at once. David Lapworth, then the Chief Engineer and now the Technical Director – in effect, the World Championship team boss – recalls an early test.

'The thing that was noticeable about Richard then, was the same sort of first impression I got from Colin McRae, although their driving styles aren't exactly the same. At that stage we aren't talking about their flat-out driving, but I actually sat in the car with both Richard and Colin the first time they drove a Legacy and it was at MIRA. What both of them had was that instinct for throttle-clutch-gearlever-steering co-ordination that some people have and some people don't. They just jump in a car and within 200 metres, they've got it sussed.

'Some people – and I'm not going to

Richard's commitment was never in doubt, but results did not always do him justice, as the Legacy was no real match for its main rival, the Sierra Cosworth. (Gavin Lodge)

mention any names – even some world champions, take several laps before they get the synchronisation of the throttle and the clutch and everything perfect – I'm talking about manuals, this is the old days, this is "historic" rallying – before they're at one with the car and everything's smooth, whereas both Colin and Richard have got that sort of instinct where that seems to come naturally to them within a couple of hundred metres, and that applies to rally cars, hire cars – whatever.'

In fact, neither of the Subaru juniors was expected to become British Champion. The clear favourite was someone with infinitely more experience than the two Legacy drivers had between them, Malcolm Wilson. He had won his first British national title in 1978 when his challengers were still in short trousers, yet despite his unquestioned ability, the Cumbrian had never quite established himself permanently in the World Championship and had returned to the British scene with a works-backed Escort Cosworth. Closely related to the Sierra, it was one of the most thoroughly developed new rally cars Ford had ever made and he had enthusiastic sponsorship from Michelin. While he would make a good yardstick for them, the Subaru drivers would do well to run him close.

It was quite typical that he had his eye on the big picture

Yet Wilson must recall 1993 with a shudder. His team was new, a fact that was soon all too obvious. On the first round, the Vauxhall Sport, Burns equalled him on the first stage and nipped ahead on the second before Malcolm asserted his seniority. That night, the Escort's wipers failed in a downpour and Burns pulled away to secure his first international victory, by 3 minutes 37 seconds. Wilson was a distant fifth. Alister McRae was second, hampered by gearbox and differential problems, but the fact remained that he had equalled his team-mate once and beaten him only twice in 15 stages – and

Richard had not been entirely satisfied with his own driving. There was no denying that it was an emphatic success.

'The only time the butterflies did start was when we were sitting in the service area before the start of the first stage and suddenly I thought, "Something is going to happen shortly that could decide the future of my whole career",' he admitted in his *Motoring News* column after the rally.

The Pirelli was fought out on the Michelin man's territory. Sure enough, Wilson was 30 seconds ahead after two stages in Kielder and more than a minute in front after the first leg. In the face of the Ford onslaught, Richard concluded that settling for second was his best bet. Nonetheless, he had coolly eased his way 41 seconds clear of a frustrated McRae, who had skidded off briefly on the second stage and damaged the rear crossmember.

Then the rally fell into Richard's lap. Wilson was stranded by electrical failure and McRae left the road for good. Despite problems with a rear hub and fluctuating hydraulic pressure in the four-wheel-drive system, he recorded his second victory of the season by no fewer than six minutes.

'I think there were people who believed Alister would be quicker than me in a Subaru straight away, but I'm not out there to prove people wrong. I'm going out there to drive fast – that's all I want to do,' he told *Motoring News* readers in his next column. His dedication to the task in hand was never in doubt, but it was entirely typical that he had an eye on the bigger picture as well and he grumbled at the lack of national coverage. If a pair of British 22-year-olds finishing first and second on the Vauxhall Sport was not a story he demanded, then what was?

All things being equal, Richard should have been no better than third on the Scottish, even if he did have a Scottish co-driver. McRae was on his patch and for Wilson Scotland is a home from home.

Richard's star quality was soon obvious. He was national champion when barely out of his teens. (Gavin Lodge)

But the following week's headlines spoke of Burns being 'one step closer to the title'. Far from turning the tide, his rivals had been powerless to prevent him from surging to yet another victory.

Wilson surrendered an early lead through gearbox failure and ended up pushing the Escort himself for a mile and a half to the end of the first forest stage. He was out of the reckoning, but the battle between the Subaru juniors was not resolved until Glenshellish, the longest and one of the roughest stages of the rally, when Alister, who was running second, got a puncture. Wilson consoled himself by setting the bulk of the fastest stage times, and the Subaru duo were ordered to hold station rather than fight each other. Richard was now in a position to settle the championship with a rally in hand, on the Ulster.

Instead, he lost his unbeaten record at last. He later admitted that he had not been especially confident, as he had never competed in Ireland before and the Ulster has a fiercesome reputation. The country lanes of the province are fast, bumpy and exceptionally slippery when wet – and a dry Ulster falls once every seven years or so. The opening stages of the second leg, south-west of Belfast, invariably cause havoc.

Sure enough, his rally came to an ignominious end, but he did not even reach the second leg. Instead, he was the most prominent victim of a punishing first day that also claimed Head and Milner when he misjudged a slippery approach to a junction and slid straight into a peat bog on the fifth stage. The Legacy was barely damaged, but stuck fast. As a result, Richard spent the second leg making gravel notes for his team-mate.

For once, Wilson's Escort ran like clockwork and he not only scored a convincing victory, but deprived Richard of the cham-

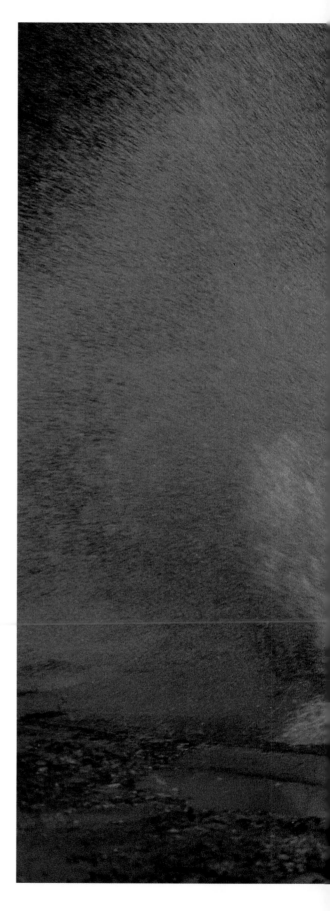

Peugeot continued to support the star it had nurtured even when he had started driving Subarus. Richard's last rally for the team was the 1992 RAC in this 200bhp 309. For once, he failed to finish.
(Gavin Lodge)

pionship lead. McRae was also in with a chance. Everything would depend on the Manx.

It wasn't quite winner takes all though. Wilson needed four registered championship contenders separating him from Burns to make sure of the crown. He was also in sufficient discomfort to need painkillers after a mammoth accident during the 1000 Lakes Rally. If Richard's concentration had faltered briefly in County Tyrone, it was not going to happen again. Beating Wilson was the goal; losing to McRae was unthinkable.

'I thought, "Right, if that's the way it's going to be, then I've got to beat him. It's as simple as that," and I just made so sure that I did everything possible. When it came to the Manx, I practised the stages 15–16 times. I was over on the Isle of Man for two weeks and I'd been over every stage without Robert. I was so, so determined to make sure we won that one.'

On the eve of the 1000 Lakes, he had had a ride in Finland with one of his boyhood heroes, Markku Alén, in one of the new works Imprezas. The terrain could scarcely be more different, but the level of knowledge and commitment required for the Manx is not unlike Finland's round of the World Championship – and the top Finns often practised alone to ensure that they had memorised every crest and curve. It was a useful insight.

After two stages on the Isle of Man, the championship was a two-horse race. McRae slammed his Legacy into a ditch and broke the suspension on the second stage, whereupon Wilson assumed control. He was no fewer than 52 seconds ahead after eight stages and starting to look very comfortable, but the island can be a vicious, unforgiving place and when he misjudged a bump, the Escort was reduced to scrap in an instant. The British title was Richard's, provided he finished.

Prodrive begged him to drive more slowly. Kenny McKinstry snatched the lead in his private Legacy. Richard was

Prodrive's junior team smiles for the cameras, (from left): Alister McRae, David Senior, Robert Reid and Richard Burns line up with the Legacys for the 1993 British International Championship. (Gavin Lodge)

told to forget about winning: let the genial lawnmower man from County Down have his moment of glory. The championship was the thing that mattered. Indeed, the team management went spectating – a near unheard-of occurrence – to make sure that Richard was taking no chances.

He dutifully eased the car away from stage starts to minimise the strain on the transmission but, as one admirer of his fluid, unflustered style put it, 'You drive 5 per cent slower and go 10 per cent faster.'

He was not letting McKinstry off the hook though and when the Ulsterman snapped a driveshaft, Richard made sure of his fourth win from five starts and his fourth championship in as many years.

At 22, he had become the youngest-ever British Rally Champion – a year younger than Colin McRae had been in 1991 – and the comparisons between the two had begun in earnest. At last, the dream that Richard Burns would become a works driver was on the point of being realised. In the heady days following his Manx triumph, all kinds of glittering international possibilities were aired. The

weeklies claimed that he might contest the Sanremo Rally, or even the 1994 French Championship, either of which would have boosted his asphalt experience. He had indisputably outgrown the British stage.

The accolades piled up. In November, he handed out the prizes for the Peugeot Challenge and then François Delecour – the winner of the Rally of Portugal and the Tour of Corsica – presented him with the British Champion's trophy. It symbolised the end of a chapter.

Sure enough, just a day after the RAC was over, Richard was on his way to the Rally of Thailand, the deciding round of the Asia-Pacific Championship. The lanky youth who had started the 1990 Peugeot Challenge in a set of overalls that Williams had given him as a birthday present would be pulling on the distinctive blue

Malcolm Wilson was the obvious favourite for the 1993 Pirelli, but once the Ford man had run into trouble, Richard demonstrated his growing mastery of the Subaru with another accomplished victory. (Gavin Lodge)

and yellow Nomex of the 555 Subaru World Championship squad for the next two, perhaps three years.

No sooner was Thailand out of the way (he finished second to his team-mate, the ebullient New Zealander, 'Possum' Bourne) than he was off to Italy for the Attilio Bettega Memorial Rally, a crowd-pleasing knock-out event linked to the Bologna Motor Show. On his first visit, he finished third, beaten only by Colin McRae and the Sanremo Rally winner, Franco Cunico – and he had beaten Colin in one of their three heats.

Yet despite his success, Richard had quietened rather than silenced his detractors. A year earlier, Colin McRae had won every round of the British series with consummate ease. He had made no attempt to dis-

Richard's 1993 record was nothing short of phenomenal. Three wins in his first three rallies in a Group A Legacy earned him a commanding championship lead and confounded a number of pre-season predictions. (Gavin Lodge)

guise his boredom at the lack of opposition, although it had not included anything like as formidable an adversary as Malcolm Wilson. The difference in style between the 1992 and the 1993 champions was piercingly apparent: Richard did not damage cars much, but the measured approach did damage of another kind, raising the hard-to-disprove suggestion that while the older McRae's blistering turn of speed was obvious, Burns's cardinal virtue was mere consistency. In different circumstances, indeed, who was to say that he would humble Alister McRae so convincingly?

On the RAC, Richard had hoped for a place in the top five. If it was not for a brief encounter with a log in Clocaenog Forest, he might have achieved his target. As it was, he came seventh, three places higher than Alister, but not exactly a threat to Juha Kankkunen, who had clinched his fourth and final World Championship in a Toyota that looked as though it had had a narrow escape from the crusher. In view of his inexperience,

Richard had put in a highly creditable performance on one of the most icy, most difficult RAC rallies in recent years – the state of Kankkunen's car proved that – but after years of nurturing aggressive Finns to whom cars were expendable, the British rally establishment expected budding stars to set the pulse racing. Colin McRae had done so and he would have had even fewer qualms with a long-term contract in his pocket.

However, Andy Moss, Prodrive's Team Manager for the 1993 British season, sees no basis for criticising the 1993 Champion. He felt the differences between Richard and Alister were obvious too.

'There was obviously a lot of rivalry and both parties appreciated the challenge. However, it has to be said (and this is probably true of Richard's career, full stop) that he is a very focused chap and therefore is committed in every way possible and there is no such thing – or certainly at that stage – of clubbing or anything else that would distract him. His focus was purely on the event and in between events, on making more of that event, or getting to know the car more or testing.

'I would say probably the biggest influence that assisted Richard at that time was David Williams. He was very good at maintaining Richard's focus and making sure that he understood the values of not only his driving, but his presentation, how he behaved, where he was seen, what he did off the circuit – all this sort of thing – and I would say that was the difference. The only real rivalry came on a couple of events when they [Burns and McRae] were very, very close. In reality, there was very little to choose between them in terms of driving performance, that's a sure thing.

'The key to it I suppose – Colin is the

The factory-entered Legacy was a big step up, but Richard had been driving powerful cars for years and defied the odds to dominate the 1993 British season. (Gavin Lodge)

The 1993 event was one of the most difficult, most hostile RAC Rallies in years and Richard had had all too little prior experience of snow. Seventh place was a more than respectable result against World Championship opposition. (Gavin Lodge)

exception; I can't think of anybody outside Colin that has really made it without good guidance. We're in a professional sport today and it's not acceptable just to be a quick lad. You've got to be presented in the right place, you've got to be put in the right position, you've got to be heard, you've got to be noticed and that does not come from just being very quick on the Plains Rally, or the Bournemouth Rally or winning the British Championship. Richard represents a perfect model in terms of what you want to achieve.'

Few men relish criticism of their driving ability, but Richard placidly accepts that consistency was the decisive factor in 1993. He's familiar with the doubters' argument.

'Well, "Malcolm [Wilson] was miles faster and then had a problem" scenario, generally, you'd have to say that was true. Malcolm blitzed us in Cumbria and he blitzed us in Scotland when he was going, but he wasn't winning the rallies, for whatever reason. Having said that, it was quite difficult for everyone to expect us to beat Malcolm, considering his record already up to that point. He'd been a Ford works driver. He'd done Finland and Greece, he'd done everything. He was miles further up the ladder than us, so to be close to him was an achievement for us and fortunately for us, his car wasn't reliable, because I'm sure he'd have won the championship otherwise.'

Wilson was by no means the first, or the last victim of Burns's nagging, unflagging consistency. As for his conqueror, he would have to get used to the idea that achieving goals only raises expectations further still.

Richard's first season as a works driver exceeded his wildest expectations. He ended the year as the youngest-ever British Rally Champion. A glittering future with Subaru looked in prospect. (Gavin Lodge)

chapter four

Weakness exposed

Richard's life was changing at dizzying speed. As he celebrated his 23rd birthday, he had become a factory driver, with a company car and a salary that was not only far in excess of anything he might have made stacking shelves, but comfortably more than he had imagined Prodrive might offer the junior member of a driving squad that also included a double World Champion, Carlos Sainz, and the sport's hottest rising star, Colin McRae.

He has a tremendous confidence in his own ability

With a regular income, he could stand on his own two feet. In 1994, he left home for the first time and moved in with his girlfriend, Belinda Jellett. Soon, they were sharing a house with some friends in Oddington, a small village north-west of Oxford in which life revolved around the pub. Richard was finding out a good deal more about women and parties, and even, belatedly, alcohol.

Belinda, who is now Human Performance Manager at Prodrive but was then working on the PR side, recalled: 'I just liked him as a person – he was kind and gentle and used to make me laugh. He was quite young then and emotional, but in a really engaging way. He would notice things or talk about things in a way that I found really interesting.

'Even in the early days, I tried to help him with his career. I always tried to encourage him to keep fit and talked things through after his rallies. The other thing that was quite interesting was that I used to get a "feeling" for exactly how he was going to perform before each rally, and nine times out of ten it was accurate! There were certain events where I absolutely knew he was going to win, such as the RAC '98 and some rallies where I knew he wasn't going to do well, like Indonesia '94 or Hong Kong–Peking '95.

'The thing that was really impressive about Richard was how he managed to pick himself up after a rally where he had an accident or made a mistake. I knew that by the time I got to speak to him, later that day or that evening, that somehow he would have justified it in his mind that it was OK. For example, that he may have made a mistake but that he had put in some storming times beforehand, so it didn't matter. He had and still has tremendous confidence in his ability.'

One of those friends, the photographer Colin McMaster, remembers the speed of that change.

'Initially, he was the ideal friend to have: a non-drinker who liked driving, which was perfect for me! But he developed a nice taste for vodka – not really much of a beer drinker. He'd go down the pub quite a lot. The more he went, the more they wanted to know about his latest overseas mission and the more he got timid about his elevation in terms of being a sports star. He found that quite difficult to handle.'

He was even more sensitive about his television image, earnestly wanting to know how he came across on camera.

His programme reflected his junior status. He was to concentrate on the Asia-Pacific Championship. He would also get a run on the RAC Rally, of course, and perhaps a drive in a Group N Subaru on the Safari. There was talk of some 'additional events' too, although they never materalised.

The six rounds of the Asia-Pacific Championship were clearly the priority, but as the Far Eastern campaign did not start until June, his first rally of the season was one of the most challenging events on the calendar, the Safari. It was not a challenge that greatly enthused Prodrive at the time. The Kenyan event might be the

stuff of legend, but that was because it was much longer and considerably more destructive than any other round of the World Championship. It therefore demanded manpower, material and money on an epic scale, including aeroplane and helicopter support, along with a separate development programme if the cars were not to be shaken to pieces. It would tie up resources Prodrive could ill-afford to spare and, as it was not compulsory for manufacturers to contest every round of the World Championship at the time, it was not part of the Anglo-Japanese team's schedule. However, the Safari carries tremendous prestige in Japan and a Subaru presence of some kind was therefore desirable. As a compromise, it was agreed that Richard would drive an Impreza WRX for a works-supported Group N team run from Japan by one of the men who had spurred Subaru to get

In 1994, Richard's horizons were widened at a bewildering speed. His first rally of the year – and only his second trip outside Europe – was the Safari, driving a Group N Impreza WRX. (McKlein)

involved in rallying in the first place, Noriyuki Koseki, a buccaneering figure with an eyepatch and an unshakeable faith in the merits of the standard car that was not always justified by events.

Richard's team-mate was the Kenyan, Patrick Njiru. Outpacing him was not a problem; getting the upper hand in the course of such a long and arduous event was another matter. Njiru was a wily operator who was not only a national hero in Kenya, a man whose public appearances triggered something akin to mass hysteria, but much respected within Subaru Tecnica International, not least because he spoke Japanese. To Richard's astonishment, reports were soon circulating that he had been driving like a lunatic in the recce, that the car would never take the punishment and that he had already rolled. There was not a grain of truth in them, but he had a shrewd idea who had probably planted the stories in the first place.

Fitness becomes an even more important concern in tropical heat. Richard confers with Prodrive's doctor at the time, David Williams.

Once the rally commenced, Richard settled into a comfortable Group N lead and he was up to fourth place after the first leg, with Njiru close behind. Then the Impreza's brakes failed at 100mph and he spun off, damaging the rear suspension. When the brakes were fixed, he was further delayed by a broken engine mounting. Even so, he was just 10 minutes behind Njiru at the finish after more than 23 hours of competitive sections, but Subaru had applied team orders and he therefore had to make do with fifth place and second in class. It was to become a familiar routine.

The Asia-Pacific series was not the obvious path to World Championship stardom, but it had a certain value nonetheless and if Prodrive regarded it as a sideshow, it certainly was not an afterthought. It is a general if not infallible rule of thumb that the FIA's regional rally championships are somewhat less demanding than the toughest European national series. Even the best-established, the European Championship, generally falls to someone the factory teams might hesitate to employ as a test driver. But

since its inception in 1987, the Asia-Pacific series had grown at a speed matching the 'tiger' economies that raised it to prominence. Frustrated by the FIA's evident reluctance to promote the World Championship, Mitsubishi was turning its firepower towards the Far Eastern contest and Subaru had a substantial presence to please its sponsor, British American Tobacco. While Richard might have harboured dreams of winning the RAC Rally or the Monte, to BAT the Hong Kong–Peking Rally and a burgeoning, chain-smoking audience was the highlight of the calendar.

From a career point of view, the main attraction for Subaru's junior was the chance to compete in Australia and New Zealand, as both events usually counted towards the World Championship. Rallies such as Thailand or Malaysia were just part of the job and the opposition, led by old stagers like 'Possum' Bourne and the Australian Ross Dunkerton, would not cause him to lose much sleep.

The reality was somewhat different. Finishing second in Thailand at the very end of 1993 had been far from easy.

'That blew my mind, because everything happened there. For a start, it was the first time I'd ever been out of Europe. It was straight after the RAC, which was a hell of a rally that year with the snow and everything. We went to Bangkok, stayed one night – flew out first class: it was all like, "Hello, I could get used to this". I'd been upgraded – and wasn't having to pay for anything.

'I got ill, straight away. I arrived there and did the recce in these standard Toyota Carinas and I thought, "This is OK. 'Possum', don't really know much about him. I know he can go quite quick, but it shouldn't be a problem. Ross Dunkerton? It won't be a problem, should be able to beat these guys." But then of course it's bloody hot, it was dusty, it was a more powerful car than I'd driven, because it was running on Avgas. There was quite a lot of expectation I think, and I nearly killed a guy on the recce as well – I hit a

New Zealand is often a home from home for British drivers and Richard was going well on his first visit, in 1994, until he crashed his works Impreza. (McKlein)

guy on a motorbike and I was whistled off at gunpoint to a police station. So I'd had the full works before the rally had even started. Everything had gone pear-shaped basically.

'Then, come the rally, it was loads rougher than anything I'd ever experienced. I'd got no idea how to go over the rough stuff. We started the rally and I was third – and well and truly third. And I thought, "This isn't going to be quite so easy". In the end, we got past Dunkerton, who was in a Lancer, and "Possum" won by a minute or something from us, but that was a bit of an eye-opener.'

Eyes open, bowels open, Richard was none too taken with the tropics. Prolonged acquaintance never converted him to local dishes, the climate, or to plantations infested with cobras, on the sound basis that they eat rats. Bourne vividly remembers his new team-mate's arrival.

Teaching him a little bit of local culture was bloody difficult!

'He was like, pretty young. And of course – don't take this wrong – all you gentlemen from England, you're hopeless bastards at travelling in those sort of places, eating the food and things like that. We tried to teach him a bit of culture, which actually was bloody difficult! As far as eating the local food, it was, "Where's TGI's and where's Pizza Hut?" Those were the only places he'd eat. It was hard for him, because the food culture there was so different to what he was used to in the UK and Robert was worse. So, it was a bit of a thing. I think they'd had a pretty good run all their time to that point and they just thought they'd clean everyone up and go home. But, it didn't happen that way.

'I only had to finish to win the championship, but in my own mind, I thought I still needed to go pretty quick and I wanted to win the rally, so we went out and we flogged them to start with and once they got used to it, it was fairly even from there to the end. But he seemed to learn pretty quick. I quite liked them both, but I thought at the time that Robert was fairly hard work. I didn't know how we'd get on over a period of time, but as it turns out, we've got on pretty good. It's just his nature and once you got used to how he was and what he was on about, really he was battling all the time the best possible deal he could get for his driver, which is what a co-driver should do, so you can't take anything away from him on those points.'

Bourne reckoned that, as far as Richard's education went, Thailand had a great deal to commend it.

'It was probably the best thing, because you've got the hardest job to start with and the rest is easy after that. He was much happier in Malaysia when we went there and stayed in town, because there was a TGI's up the road. It was the food that got to him more than anything else. To me, he's matured a lot and he was always quick, wasn't he? There was never going to be a drama with that.'

That is a generous tribute from someone who had been forced to fight tooth and nail to retain his place at Subaru when Prodrive came on the scene and cannot have relished the arrival of yet another team-mate who was expected to progress to greater things. Richard had to learn that being quick on home ground did not count for much on the opposite side of the globe and the rallies themselves were deceptively difficult. It was not just the stifling heat, although 555's dark blue colour scheme only made that worse. When it rained, the plantation tracks offered as much grip as wet soap and, regardless of the weather, they were often brutally rough. Bourne and Dunkerton knew the score only too well and after the former clinched the 1993 title, Mitsubishi decided to send Kenneth Eriksson – the ultra-determined Swede whom Richard had watched with such admiration testing a Toyota six years previously – to bolster its attack for 1994.

To make Richard's life more difficult still, the rally world was inclined to underestimate Eriksson, never mind Bourne and struggling to beat them did not exactly burnish his reputation. He did not have much luck either. He was leading the Rally of Indonesia after the first leg, which was no mean feat on only his second rally in the Far East, but retired when the studs sheared and a rear wheel bounded into the undergrowth the next morning. Richard suspects that he is doubted even now, but swears that he hit nothing. To his way of thinking, there is no sense in lying to a team anyway, however tempting it may appear in the heat of the moment.

New Zealand promised better things. It brought true World Championship opposition and it is not only one of the rallies that drivers enjoy the most, but the event which most closely resembles the RAC. Richard recorded some excellent stage times, including third quickest on that most exacting of North Island stages, the relentless succession of corners known as the Motu Road, beating Kankkunen, Eriksson and Vatanen, amongst others. However, he crashed a stage later and in a week when none of his team-mates finished, Colin McRae, the 'Motumeister' himself, saved the day for Subaru with an accomplished victory. It was July and Richard had yet to score an Asia-Pacific Championship point.

He redeemed himself with second in Malaysia, dutifully if reluctantly finishing behind Bourne when the Mitsubishis fell by the wayside, and fifth place in Australia – another fast, difficult event, on which newcomers rarely do well. A month later, he was second on a rally that he came to loathe, the Hong Kong–Peking. A magnificent, anachronistic adventure to some, a reminder of the days when major rallies were conceived on the grand scale and border crossings were a matter of routine, Richard found it tedious at best, exasperating at worst and it invariably strained relations with his co-driver. At the insistence of the Chinese authorities, a lengthy recce was carried out in convoy, the road sections were interminable, the hotels unpredictable and there was not a

For a works crew, it is usually best to stay out of the mechanics' way at service points. Richard and Robert Reid make themselves at home on some jerry cans while running repairs are made to their Subaru.

Western-style restaurant between Hong Kong and Peking. Thrown into close proximity in trying circumstances, Richard and Robert got on one another's nerves. After a week in China, even Robert's habit of buttering his toast right to the edge was more than Richard could stand.

In 1994, there was little opposition and the rally itself was not a great deal more entertaining than the recce. The Mitsubishis failed again and championship requirements dictated that Richard finished second rather than battling it out with 'Possum'.

All that obedience was soon forgotten on Richard's one European outing of the year. The first day of the RAC rarely counted for much then, as the spectator-orientated stages around stately homes and race tracks bore no relation to the much longer, more challenging forest stages to follow. Once the forests began, Richard at last had a chance to show his mettle, on a rally he knew well and with no team orders to consider. He was second quickest on the first forest stage, in Hamsterley and fastest Subaru driver, three seconds quicker than Colin McRae and 25 faster than the team's world title contender, Carlos Sainz.

It's that little bit of luck the two of us came together

It was a source of reassurance as much as satisfaction, but Richard provided only a glimpse of his potential. An uncharacteristic slip two stages later in Kielder led to an abrupt encounter with a rock that smashed the rear suspension. There was not much sympathy on offer. Sainz's championship rival, Didier Auriol, had all but squandered his title hopes by breaking his Toyota's front suspension on the first day in Chatsworth and Subaru needed every car it had to keep the Frenchman as far down the order as possible. The last thing it had wanted was the team apprentice suffering a rush of blood to the head when the rally had scarcely begun.

Back in the Far East, for his last rally of the year, Richard was second again in Thailand, but this time a good deal closer to Eriksson, 24 seconds in arrears. He was third in the championship behind Bourne and Eriksson, and far from disgraced. But it had not turned out quite as he had imagined when he had headed for Bangkok in first class the year previously.

The new season brought a significant change. Williams had grown frustrated and disenchanted. He had dabbled in driver management, not just with Richard, but with the younger of the Manx Higgins brothers, David, and concluded that he was not cut out for it.

'Richard learnt a lot that year. I learnt a lot that year. I learnt I didn't want to be part of rallying as a business, so I stepped back from anything to do with it as a business and I'm never going to wear team kit ever again. I'm going to be totally on Richard's side, whatever team he's on. I don't want to be part of any team, because when you wear team kit, you can't argue against the team. I used to argue with everybody and they'd just say, "Tough luck". If you are independent, you are independent. That's very important.'

Williams also felt that at works team level, Richard needed a manager with better contacts in World Championship circles and a proven track record. Accordingly, he approached Mike Greasley, a former *Motoring News* editor whose stable included Kankkunen, Eriksson, Stig Blomqvist, Martin Brundle and Mika Salo. Greasley, who was also secretary of the World Rally Teams Association, had got involved in the sport before Richard was born and was renowned not simply for his contacts, but his negotiating skills. Terms were agreed in February 1995.

The new arrangement did not mean that Williams was turning his back on Burns. On the contrary, the two remain close friends. He still attends rallies occasionally, although he has taken to racing himself, in a Mallock clubmans car. It would be a strange week in which they do not speak at least twice and Richard usually turns up at the Williams household over Christmas. But Williams had passed up his last opportunity to rake in a serious return for his time and trouble. There are all kinds of instances of young, naïve sportsmen and musicians falling in with older, more worldly advisers, but precious few that parallel the singular relationship between Williams and Burns.

'I've never made any money out of it. It's always cost me money. Money isn't the answer to everything in life,' Williams stated.

'To explain myself, in my work I've never ever tried to be successful. All I've tried to do is be a designer. We don't advertise, we don't have any brochures. We try to do a good, old-fashioned job and we get referrals for it. And it's so old-fashioned to lots of people, but to me it seems totally normal that you help people. You go rallying not to beat people, you go rallying and racing to enjoy yourself. The reason you work is you try and do your job as well as you can do it. You don't set off to make money. And in my job, which people don't see, I've started off lots and lots of young designers – probably five or

six of them – who are now successful in business, so it's not unusual for me to help people, and I like helping people.

'It's far more rewarding than getting money. Money is just something that comes and goes. Friendship, doing things – those sort of things, I mean – the pleasure I've got out of helping Richard is just so immense and the places I've been and the things I've done, it's fantastic, absolutely fantastic, and I would never ever dream of making a penny out of Richard. Anything that he does, I think he knows 120 per cent that, whatever happens, I'll always be there for him, and Gordon will be and the boys will be there. It's a really nice feeling and money doesn't give you the same feeling.'

It is a genuine sentiment. Williams's company, Genesis, derives a good deal of its income from equipping motorhomes and hospitality enclosures in Formula 1.

His son's career has given Richard's father Alex the perfect excuse for the occasional foray to an exotic destination. The two are pictured together in Thailand.

But given a choice between watching the Monaco Grand Prix from a yacht in the harbour and spending his own money racing his own car before a tiny audience back home, Williams chooses the latter. He has never advertised in any sense of the term and while he would no doubt feel uncomfortable at being portrayed as Richard's saviour, there is no false modesty either. He agrees that Richard Burns probably would not have become a professional rally driver without his help, but promptly adds that successful drivers are born, not made.

'You can tell people and you have to shout at them or force them to do something, but to a certain extent with Richard, you told him once, you point him in the right direction and off he goes. I can't manufacture that again. You have to have someone who's got that in the first place. Richard wouldn't have been able to do it commercially without me, but I wouldn't have been able to do it to anyone else apart from Richard and it's that little bit of luck the two of us came together. And the third person who should always be included is Robert, because Robert is fantastic, and Richard wouldn't go as fast without him as a co-driver.'

Richard is in no doubt of the debt he owes Williams.

'It is an extraordinary thing, that shocks quite a few people. Now, it's friendship. Then, it was master and apprentice, I suppose. I used to just do whatever he told me to do and never questioned anything and, well, that was it. I always used to do it. I didn't have any idea of what I should be doing anyway, apart from what he told me and if he said, "Richard, you've got to paint the wheels on the Nissan Patrol, because they've got a bit of rust on," I would go and paint the wheels on the Nissan Patrol, full stop. It wasn't like, "Oh, I can't be bothered to do that".

Heat and dust are not the only Safari hazards. Richard's second visit to Kenya got off to a promising start and he was running in third place in 1995 in a Group N Impreza until he crashed into some spectators' cars. (McKlein)

That's just what I did. And if the car then wasn't clean enough or tidy enough or anything, I would get a load of shit.'

Greasley was concerned that, in his eagerness to learn, Richard was admirably ready to listen to advice, but not quite so adept at sifting it. He told him to listen less – but that he should always listen to David Williams.

It is perhaps stranger still that Williams is admired by team managers. They tend to regard driver managers as a necessary evil at best, a stain on humanity at worst, yet Prodrive's Chairman, David Richards, has nothing but praise for Williams.

'David has been not just a great friend to him, but he's been a very level-headed, sensible person. You see so many other people involved in drivers' careers – they tend to be parental influences – and in the main, they do extraordinary things at an early stage and then they overstep the mark or they seek the limelight. David has done none of those things. David has done all that's necessary for Richard and stood back when it's not been necessary, and he couldn't have asked for a more

Like most drivers, Richard's taste for speed isn't slaked by the job alone. He is one of a number of the World Championship contenders to relax on a jet ski. (McKlein)

loyal, more appropriate person to have got him to this stage.'

But on stage, life was getting no easier. Richard's 1994 results did not merit a bigger programme in Prodrive's view and in 1995 he contested just six rallies, a hotchpotch of World and Asia-Pacific Championship events that guaranteed that he was never the team's priority. In fact, there was so much slack in his 1995 campaign that he was told he was free to drive for other teams as well if he wished, and Reid even investigated the possibility of their contesting the British Championship as well, with Renault in a Clio Williams. While the French team was new to Britain, it was ambitious and had money to spend. However, it also wanted an exclusive deal and there was of course no sense in sacrificing the Subaru drive.

Richard had plenty of time to work on his fitness and to dwell on other aspects of his career. In a *Motoring News* column, he revealed that he had put on 7kg through 'training and good eating'. To his housemates' surprise, he would spend evenings watching in-car videos to help him learn stages. There was also plenty of time to brood. The lack of opportunity and lack of success led to growing disenchantment on both sides and it was not long before rumours began to circulate that Prodrive would not be taking up its option on the third year of the deal signed at the end of 1993.

Richards was under pressure from Subaru's tyre supplier, Pirelli, to make more use of the Italian driver, Piero Liatti, a former European Champion who had also been one of Lancia's preferred test drivers. Furthermore, Burns's results were not strengthening his case. Whenever comparisons were drawn with Colin McRae, they were rarely favourable. Some members of the team observed that McRae had been fortunate, in that the team was developing the car when he had burst on to the scene and could therefore settle for a driver who also had plenty to learn. It was bad luck on Richard that Subaru now expected a good deal more, but then nobody said life was fair.

His first appearance of the season, on the Rally of Portugal in March, produced a magnificent win for Sainz, but only seventh for Richard. He had not been given sub-standard equipment, but he was never on the same tyres as his team-mates and that made an appreciable difference on an exceptionally wet and muddy event that is noted for its constant surface changes at the best of times.

It had been another memorable experience, Richard estimating that there were more spectators on the recce than there would be on a British Championship rally, but in his *Motoring News* column, he confessed that he had never driven at more than 80 per cent.

'You were never able to get into a rhythm, because the stages never flowed. There was never a stage where I felt I could have a real go, in the knowledge I wouldn't have a problem,' he complained.

A month later, he was part of Koseki's Group N Safari squad once more and was

Once again, New Zealand promised much, but delivered little. Richard looked on course for a strong points finish until he fell foul of one of the fords on the Motu Road. (McKlein)

going well in the first leg, rising to a highly creditable third place until he had a bizarre accident. He was travelling at well over 100mph when he shot over a crest to find two spectators' cars parked almost in the middle of the track. The Safari is run on roads open to all traffic and accidents with non-participants are by no means unheard of, but on this occasion the culprits were well aware that they were on the rally route and might possibly have pulled to the side before discussing where they would go next.

'I was in an Impreza and it was a Vivio-sized gap,' Richard reflected. After that, neither he nor the spectators were going anywhere.

Another three months ebbed past before he was next called up, for New

Zealand – and even then, he was needed primarily because Sainz had broken his shoulder in a mountain bike accident. If it was not for that, he would have languished on the substitutes' bench until the Hong Kong–Peking in October. Again, Richard was going well despite his lack of match practice, holding a place in the top five until he got to the Motu. Colin McRae (who clinched his New Zealand hat trick and laid the foundations of his world title assault) took the ford in the middle flat out and surfed through on the sump-guard. His team-mate did the prudent thing and lifted the accelerator a fraction: the nose dipped a little and water gushed through the engine bay, ripping the alternator drive belt off. The Impreza would have reached the end of the stage on the remaining current in the battery, but the belt also drove the water pump and he was forced to retire when the engine cooked itself.

I was worried about my job, worried about my future

Richard felt that guidance from the team was inadequate or non-existent.

'That was one complaint I did have at that time – or I didn't know I had it, because it was always too late – but I always used to get told what I should have done afterwards rather than before … I just always had in the back of my mind, "If I don't finish, no one's going to want to employ me."'

He had some reason to be worried. Asked how he rated Richard Burns, one senior Prodrive figure at the time replied that he might make a good number three. It was a belittling compliment in 1995, when the biggest teams ran three cars. These days, they run two.

Five years later, no one at Prodrive, Richards least of all, was likely to make disparaging remarks about the man who had become the star driver, but his view of Burns's progress seemed fair comment.

'If I'm honest about it – and in hindsight – he probably didn't get the proper opportunity at that time. He was very much the junior. He was in a team with Carlos Sainz and Colin McRae, and probably he was at a point in his career where we should have lavished more attention on him.

'But inevitably, he was going to have a dip in his fortunes at some point in time – and I'm not for one minute making excuses for him – but I think those two issues probably just coincided,' he observed.

Williams suggested that Richard might like to see a sports psychologist and he turned to Phil Fearon, who had worked with the now-defunct British Junior Rally Team in the mid-1980s and with a variety of other sportsmen, including James Hunt and the motorcyclist, Wayne Gardner.

'When everyone said, "Yeah, he can drive, but he's not going to win anything," that was when I was worried about a lot of factors. I was worried about my job, worried about my future. I was disappointed with myself sometimes and perhaps didn't believe in myself. Those things combined meant that I wasn't performing to my best, for sure. That changed a lot. You know I went to see Phil Fearon. That helped. That started the turnaround, I would say. In a nutshell, what I learnt to do was forget all the things that can go wrong and just to think about the things that are good and why I could set fastest times, and what I do to set that fastest time and then you start answering any questions for yourself, basically. He was asking me a lot of questions that just made me realise how daft you were being – the really common sense stuff that makes a difference. Think about the good bits, not the bad bits: simple,' Richard explained.

In general terms, Fearon saw nothing remarkable in Richard's outlook at the time.

'I do think that any top sportsman is increasingly worried about his own performance and that tends to be on the introversion [side], where they're looking at themselves rather than their opponents and their equipment. Some blame the machinery and some look inwardly and say, "Is it the machinery or is it me also?"

One of the things I've found is introversion in quite a high number of rally drivers,' he said.

The visits to a psychologist and the snatching at good stage times as crumbs of comfort on otherwise disappointing rallies might be seen as evidence that Richard had reached the limits of his ability; the consistency that had propelled him so smoothly to the top in Britain would not suffice on the world stage, just as his detractors had suspected in 1993. The best drivers lack neither raw speed nor self-belief, they might have argued.

Indeed, *Motoring News* sounded far from persuaded that he was a World Champion in the making in its 1995 seasonal review.

'He still needs to find a little extra pace at World Championship level compared to other drivers battling to join the first division, such as Freddy Loix and Thomas Rådström,' the reviewer suggested.

In early December, that came across not so much as an opinion but as a rebuke. At the time, Richard had yet to sign a contract for 1996, Loix – a Belgian who had shown similar promise – was one of the drivers he feared the most and a cataclysm had burst over the sport. A month previously Toyota had been caught red-handed on the Catalonia Rally, running illegal, adjustable turbo restrictors that flagrantly breached the 34mm limit and offered a substantial power boost. The FIA treated the infringement with unusual savagery and banned Toyota Team Europe for 12 months; the fact that the team boss, Ove Andersson, was one of the most dogged critics of its failure to improve World

The works Subarus were near-unbeatable in the second half of 1995. Richard played his full part, his third place on the RAC Rally that autumn being his best World Championship result at that time. (McKlein)

Rally Championship television coverage was no doubt entirely coincidental.

The FIA's exemplary justice left the drivers' market awash. Kankkunen, Auriol and Sainz – who had planned to move back to Toyota for 1996 – were thrown out of work, along with Armin Schwarz. They had seven world titles and more than 50 World Championship rally wins between them. Yet Richard was neither out of work for 1996, nor in as bad a predicament as he perhaps imagined in those idle months earlier in the season.

In the first instance, his results improved noticeably in the closing weeks of 1995. Mitsubishi triumphed on the Hong Kong–Peking, but Richard came third, beating Bourne for the first time. If he had not slid off on one of the southern stages and got stuck on a concrete lip for several minutes, he would have presented the Lancers with a much sterner challenge.

I had quite a strong feeling that Richard was going to be good

On the RAC, he was an accomplished third, no match for the inspired McRae perhaps, but then Colin tore through the forests and even Sainz's defences like a tornado to become the youngest-ever World Rally Champion. After a fumbling start when he splayed the front wheels against a log on the first stage at Tatton Park, Richard had done everything the team could have wished, playing a full part in securing its second consecutive sweep of the top three places.

Days later, he was third in Thailand, but this was certainly his most impressive performance in the Far East so far. Tommi Mäkinen was the victor, but just five seconds spanned the first three and Richard finished one paltry second behind Eriksson. If he had not been held up for a time in dust, he might well have beaten the Mitsubishi duo.

In fact, it had not taken that autumn show of promise to convince other teams that they wanted Burns. Subaru had persuaded Eriksson, the new Asia-Pacific Champion, to swap sides by promising him an extensive World Championship programme and Mitsubishi badly wanted someone with Asia-Pacific experience and a useful turn of speed to fill the breach. It would be fair to say that it wanted someone cheap as well and, following the TTE ban, value for money remained very much on Richard's side, but the team management was keenly aware that even the most experienced and talented newcomers often needed time to adapt to the peculiar demands of rallying in South East Asia. Mitsubishi was looking somewhat further ahead in any case.

Negotiations proceeded smoothly. Like Subaru's, Mitsubishi's rally team is as British as scattered showers and sunny intervals; the premises are in Rugby and most of the workforce is British. Its Team Manager, Phil Short, a former co-driver who had accompanied everyone from his Ford counterpart in the mid-1990s, John Taylor, to Walter Röhrl and David Llewellin, approached Burns and Reid in Hong Kong.

'I had certainly quite a strong feeling about Richard that he was going to be good. The first time I'd come across him was when I was invited to be one of the judges on the Shell Scholarship. Richard finished second and I felt he was actually the best candidate on offer, but my particular responsibility was assessing the co-drivers and I have to say I was very impressed with Robert Reid on that day, and I think I was quoted in the press as saying I thought he had World Championship potential. So as far as I was concerned, Richard was very much the right choice and Japan fairly rapidly endorsed that,' he said.

'Sure, there were other, more experienced drivers available at the time and certainly our telephones were ringing. Maybe to some observers, Richard was perceived as just a bit of a journeyman driver – certainly some way behind McRae, whose way into the sport was quite different – and therefore he wasn't particularly highly regarded, but we could see the potential. Japan's thinking on drivers has always tended to be to look for the young, up and coming drivers rather than take the old establishment.'

It was an enticing, but risky deal. It was centred on the Asia-Pacific series in the first instance and while Richard was being offered a substantial pay rise that took him comfortably into the six-figure bracket, it wasn't a king's ransom by World Championship standards. On the other hand, he was being presented with a three-year deal by a team with a highly competitive car, managed by a pair of shrewd, seasoned campaigners; the Director, Andrew Cowan, was a double winner of the London–Sydney Rally who had driven for everyone from British Leyland to Rootes and Mercedes. Richard would get the chance to develop at his own pace. Even if he spent most of his time in the Far East at first, it looked a better bet than the alternatives.

Ford also took an interest. Richard considered it and, to Ford's surprise, turned down a test drive at Boreham. He replied that the team knew enough about him and he knew enough about the car. Neither side was going to learn much more if he trundled an Escort Cosworth across Boreham's crumbling Tarmac.

There were other reasons for approaching Ford warily. Its past treatment of British drivers bordered on the cannibal and when a member of the team told Richard that he would do better to look elsewhere, he rejected the offer. He still had a choice: either Mitsubishi – or Subaru. At a late stage, Prodrive recanted. Sue Greasley, Mike's wife, found herself fielding a conference call with Richards and the Team Manager, John Spiller. Subaru realised that without Burns, its own Asia-Pacific team would be a little short of depth and on reflection, perhaps

The end of 1995 was one long celebration for everyone involved with Subaru and Prodrive. Richard poses with his house-mates (right to left), Colin McMaster, Fiona Spragg and Belinda Jellett.

Richard's first stint with Subaru ended with the Rally of Thailand and almost produced another victory. He was only a handful of seconds behind the winning Mitsubishis. (McKlein)

it had underestimated his potential.

As Lapworth said, 'On most of the rallies, you would see trends where his times would generally improve and he would maybe identify certain stages where he felt confident or he had been there before and he would put in very good times. It wasn't exactly like certain other characters that we could mention where he ran consistently a second a kilometre off the pace. He may have been finishing fifth-sixth-seventh in World Championship rallies – generally he was cautious, learning the

ropes – but every now and again you would see, "That's a pretty good time, that was nearly on the pace, that one".'

Richard was not mollified by Prodrive's show of contrition.

'They then offered me more money, they offered me more rallies. But I eventually said no, because I would still be third driver. They started moving the goalposts up and up and up. I said, "If you wanted to keep me, why didn't you offer me that money in the first place?" I just thought the only reason they wanted me was to stop me going to Mitsubishi, rather than wanting me at Subaru.'

On 12 December, Richard signed a contract with Mitsubishi, as team-mate for a quick but erratic Finn, Tommi Mäkinen.

chapter five

'Tommi says this is better'

As the Ralliart mechanics took the sledgehammers to Richard's Lancer, his first season with Mitsubishi was in much the same state of disrepair as the car's boot. It was mid-June, he had yet to finish a rally with his new team and he appeared to be on the brink of his third successive retirement owing to an accident.

Short looked solemn. Even if the damage could be repaired sufficiently to keep the car in the running, there was the Rally of New Zealand to consider six weeks later and thousands of miles away. If this particular Lancer could not be straightened, Richard would not be going to New Zealand. The team did not have an infinite supply of cars.

> **It was not even as if he had looked like winning**

Richard sought refuge and reassurance in a chat with Williams. He had misjudged a sharp bend at the end of a long straight and spun the car tail-first into a palm tree. He had not lost much time, but that was beside the point.

On the Asia-Pacific opener in Thailand in March, he had been right behind Colin McRae and had just clipped a few seconds off the World Champion when he slid wide, nicked a tree and crashed heavily.

These things happen. At least he had been going well at the time. Nonetheless, the accident had badly undermined his confidence and Indonesia, newly elevated to the World Championship, was pretty much the rally he least wanted to find next on the schedule. To make matters worse, a downpour had turned the opening stages south of Medan into a quagmire and staying on the road at all was a challenge. Richard failed it, sliding just wide enough on the very first stage to smash the Lancer's lightweight front bumper and the vulnerable cooling systems behind it. He had done little harm to the bodyshell, but he had split the oil cooler and predictably, the engine failed two stages later.

By Malaysia, the mechanics were none too impressed. It was hot enough just lolling in the shade that day near Port Dickson, without putting up with a new driver who arrived with a reputation for consistency and justified that reputation only in the sense that he consistently launched the car off the road. It was not even as if he had looked like winning. Their old driver, Eriksson, looked to be settling in comfortably at Subaru and a superb display on stages that were often viciously slippery had earned him a lead of almost a minute.

Richard steadied himself. If the boot

had been crushed another two inches, the bodyshell would have been scrap. It was none too pretty, but he was still in and still on course for New Zealand too. It was a chaotic rally, even by Malaysian standards: mopeds rode up and down the plantation tracks at will, marshals failed to appear and the stewards cancelled stage after stage on safety grounds. Eventually, the works teams ended up providing mechanics to marshal junctions. So many stages would have been cancelled otherwise that the rally would not have counted for Asia-Pacific Championship points.

A fortnight later, Richard was fourth on his first attempt at the Rally of Argentina (a fine showing, as he felt ill for much of the rally) and later that July, the complexion of his season changed entirely. New Zealand always looked a good bet: after two previous visits, he knew the lie of the land and the opposition was not as strong as usual. Under the lamentable and unlamented rotation system then in use, each World Championship rally was demoted one year in three, in which it counted only towards the F2, two-wheel-drive series. Naturally, the most powerful teams either ignored such rallies or rested their top drivers. It was New Zealand's turn for demotion in 1996 and although Subaru and Mitsubishi were present in some force on the trail of Asia-Pacific points, Subaru did not send McRae and Ford skipped the rally altogether.

Richard faced Mäkinen and Eriksson nevertheless, as well as Subaru's Italian, Liatti. Gradually, the rally turned in his favour. Mäkinen's early visits to New Zealand rarely justified the flight and this was no exception. He thundered into the lead during the first leg, then into a tree stump while cutting a corner and wrenched a front wheel off, retiring at the end of the stage.

On recent form, that should have tilted the odds towards Eriksson. He was the most experienced of the visitors and, while the Impreza was reckoned to lack the Lancer's power, its proven agility ought to have compensated on North Island's twisty, heavily cambered roads. Instead, the Swede tied himself in knots altering suspension settings, leaving Richard to face Liatti. There was not much in it after the first leg, the Italian holding a narrow advantage, but Richard

Far Eastern rallies are generally fought out on punishing dirt tracks in lush plantations. Richard achieved his first finish for Mitsubishi in Malaysia, despite thudding into a palm tree. (McKlein)

took command on the long run through the Motu and the Matawhai Gorge and, by the time Eriksson was prevailed upon to return to the original settings, his Mitsubishi replacement had an unassailable lead.

It was not exactly a World Championship win – more of a half pint than a full measure – but it was most definitely a result worth toasting even so. It was Richard's first victory outside Britain and indeed, his first anywhere since the 1993 Manx. It had been a very lengthy barren spell indeed for a young man in a hurry, but it had gone a long way towards justifying Ralliart's faith. Back home, the party in Oxford continued well into the small hours.

Yet Richard remained ill at ease in the Lancer Evo III. It was generally reckoned to be the best rally car in the world, at least on loose surfaces. Its engine was ideally suited to the more restrictive turbocharger rules introduced in 1995, which effectively cut maximum revs as well as power,

At the third attempt, Richard had some luck in New Zealand at last. A superb drive yielded his first victory outside Britain and his first for Mitsubishi. (McKlein)

but there was no denying that it was tricky to drive. In part, that was because of the rear suspension geometry. The rear track narrowed under braking, which made the car liable to snap sideways, but it had a good deal more to do with Ralliart's unique four-wheel drive system. Whether they were conventional and mechanical, viscous couplings that relied on a silicon-based fluid, or hydraulic, all Mitsubishi's rivals used clutch-based differentials incorporating plates designed to lock. Mitsubishi's electro-magnetic transmission has clutch plates, but it operated in a very different manner, as Richard explained.

'Basically, the diffs in the Mitsubishi don't lock solidly under braking. They do now, but they didn't then. The theory was the freer the diffs were, the more power you could get through to the road and the less loss you had. But unfortunately, it meant that it was not the easiest car to drive, because it meant it would lock up wheels under braking, which massively affected your confidence. Plus the way Tommi had the car set up, if you didn't have full power through the corner, then the diffs again wouldn't lock up and my driving style is such that I play with the car in the corner quite a lot.'

Even to Mitsubishi's engineers, Mäkinen's driving style is occasionally a source of wonder. Like many Nordic drivers, he is a committed left-foot braker, but he has evolved an all-or-nothing technique in which the accelerator is stabbed to the bulkhead and the car's cornering attitude is controlled with the brakes. Even so, in full cry he generates so much braking force that one engineer assumed the equipment was broken the first time he took data.

It is a generation removed from four-wheel drive's early days with the Quattro. Electronics can be harnessed to programme a range of factors into the transmission's behaviour, with a crucial impact on the handling. In Mäkinen's case, turbo boost is one of the key measurements. Richard soon decided that Eriksson's settings were preferable and wanted throttle position to be the overriding input.

It was not necessarily easy to persuade the team that his wishes were worth considering, for in 1996, Mäkinen took the rally world by storm and a number two driver must have seemed almost a luxury rather than a necessity. He had made certain of a truncated, nine-round World Championship by September with two ral-

lies to spare and at the time of writing, he remains the only driver to have won more than half the World Championship rallies in a season.

'With Mitsubishi, it was a bit difficult, because you were always working against, "Well, Tommi says this is better". I know that I always ran a different diff setting from Tommi, Tarmac or gravel – always different, because I couldn't get on with his. I always found the car so much easier to drive when I had my own setting. I didn't have confidence then, but everything I said was correct,' Richard commented.

At Ralliart, they remember the grumbling and argue that the final compromise was an adaptation of both car and Richard's driving style, but any professional driver has to learn to fight his corner. Ultimately, being grateful for what you're given is no recipe for success.

Richard generously describes the Evo III as 'a classic', even though he admits that he never quite came to terms with it.

Almost three years of doubt and disappointment were triumphantly banished on the 1996 Rally of New Zealand, Richard joining the distinguished array of British drivers to have won the event, which includes his team boss, Andrew Cowan. (McKlein)

Sure enough, while Mäkinen flayed the opposition as he took a crushing victory and the title in Australia, Richard steered his way to fifth place. The fact that he was closing on McRae during the final leg was only taken as further evidence that the deposed World Champion's confidence was shattered after a tempestuous season in which he had crashed three times and been fined US$75,000 by the FIA for running over some spectators in Argentina.

In some respects, Richard was lucky to see the finish in Perth at all. On perhaps the wettest Rally Australia ever, the water crossing at the foot of the famous Bunnings Forest 'steps' was so deep that it claimed his Mitsubishi, along with both works Fords and Eriksson's Subaru, while McRae had had to be pushed through it. Rather than have most works crews wiped out in freakish circumstances, the organisers decided that cars could be towed to the nearby service area. Even so, Richard's engine was coaxed into life only in the nick of time.

Occasionally, the frustration was too much to conceal. Richard has a reputation as one of the calmest, most rational drivers on the World Championship trail, but on the last Hong Kong–Peking, his self-control momentarily deserted him. Midway through the fourth leg of the week-long marathon, he sprang from the car, strode away and bawled abuse across the valley. The mechanics went about their tasks in silence.

Richard was angry with himself rather than the team. He had been jostling for the lead. He had just spun and although the car was barely damaged, he had crimped a turbo pipe and lost power. He complained bitterly that a Subaru would never have spun in the circumstances, but it was no use. Liatti had rolled his Impreza long since, Eriksson had launched the other works Subaru down a ravine earlier that morning and Mitsubishi no longer had any opposition. He knew what would

He sprang out, strode away and bawled abuse across the valley

happen next. He would be obliged to accept second behind his Finnish team-mate.

It would have been a little hard to take under any circumstances, but doubly so when that team-mate was not Mäkinen, but Ari Vatanen. There are all kinds of reasons why Vatanen is justly a rallying legend, from winning the 1981 World Championship to returning successfully to the sport following his horrific accident in Argentina in 1985; his driving style remains as spectacular as ever and he is never lost for a quote. But to Richard, Ari was the old generation, someone who hadn't won a World Championship rally for 11 years. If he could not beat the old trooper, legend or no, when was he going to get the better of Mäkinen or McRae?

Sure enough, Mitsubishi imposed team orders and both drivers ignored them.

'The next stage after that they were still going at it hammer and tongs and starting to knock pieces off the cars, so we had quite strong words with both of them after that. Richard wasn't happy about it. He was almost in tears, to be honest,' Short remembered.

'He knew I was going to impose the instructions to hold station. He just made the mistake at the wrong time. That was one of the harsh realities of life, which I'm afraid he had to learn. The main thing there was that we clinched the Asia-Pacific Manufacturers' Championship. Nowadays maybe that doesn't seem all that big, but to Japan it was their main objective and we achieved that, so that certainly helped our cause for what was to come.'

Richard had another three days of driving with gritted teeth to look forward to. There was no catching Eriksson for the drivers' crown, but as it turned out, the rally nearly fell into his lap at the last gasp, when Vatanen's car cracked its block and he came within seconds of collecting road penalties into the bargain at one of the last time controls. By the end, Richard had regained his good humour and, while the finish ceremony unfolded a few hundred

Happiness is driving a works Mitsubishi. (McKlein)

yards away, he joined the mechanics in what was probably the only game of cricket ever played in Tiananmen Square.

As usual, China had soured relations with Reid and within weeks, Richard was actively seeking a new co-driver. Their last rally of the season, Catalonia, had been a qualified success until the final stage. After losing a chunk of time with a gearbox problem in the second of the three legs, they had clawed their way back to 10th place. It was perfectly respectable, given their earlier problems, that the Evo III was never much of an asphalt car – even Mäkinen was no better than fifth – and that they had not contested an all-Tarmac rally of any kind since 1993. Then Reid made a momentary but vital error reading the pace notes and they crashed into the trees at high speed.

The initial reports were confused and Cowan was furious. What had the young man been thinking of, launching the car off the road with a good result almost in the bag? When they got back to the service area in Lloret de Mar, a mortified Reid made no excuses. He informed the team that he was prepared to resign. At that moment, Richard might have welcomed it, but no one else – neither Ralliart management, nor Williams, nor the Greasleys – was in favour.

'Both Andrew and I felt that Robert was one of Richard's strengths, and one that he should keep and bury whatever trivial differences they had, because we saw that Robert was quite a strong personality in the car, very good tactically, very well organised, a very sort of level-headed, down to earth chap who did a good job so far as we were concerned. Looking at that particular incident, we watched the in-car over and over and listened to the notes. I think at that time Richard himself was probably over-complicating his notes and I think he realised that as well. Having watched subsequent in-cars, he does seem

The Lancer Evo III was never at its best on asphalt. Richard gave a good account of himself on the 1996 Catalonia Rally nonetheless, only to crash heavily near the end. (McKlein)

to have simplified things a bit. Although there's always a tendency for drivers to put more in, I think he realised then he was perhaps over-loading Robert and himself with the amount of information that was being required,' Short stated.

Williams is in full agreement: 'Over the years, there's been many times when they've nearly split apart and it's been my duty to keep them together. I cannot even imagine how much my bills have been trying to keep the two of them together. Robert is fantastic and he is equally as good as Richard is. He's a co-driver on acid. He makes all the other co-drivers look like they're not doing anything. He's got miles more notes than everybody else, because Richard wants more notes.

'Post-China, in the car for two or three weeks, they always wanted to split up. And then everybody would be on the 'phone to me over the next two or three months, and then we'd try and get them to go on different 'planes, so they'd have something to talk about; but Richard wouldn't be able to function with another co-driver.'

Spain is Sainz country and the crowds are routinely vast. Richard threads his Lancer through an eager throng. (McKlein)

Richard asserts that there was not a great deal for Robert to spit out on that fateful corner in Catalonia, but concedes that there is an excellent case for maintaining the partnership otherwise.

'Professionally, he could be a bit fitter, which he knows, but apart from that, you can't fault him. I would hate to have his job. I cannot imagine how difficult being a World Championship co-driver is, because if you get asked for your autograph nine or ten times, only one person will say, "Can I have Robert's as well?" And it's the same with all the co-drivers. It is a thankless task for a male to be sat next to another male who gets miles more attention than they do. To understand what that must be like, I can't imagine. Because he does an amazing job: preparation is probably better than any other co-driver, his pace note reading, writing, delivery is probably better than any other co-driver.

'I have quite a lot of information, probably because I am still, apart from Freddy Loix, the youngest and most inexperienced of all the drivers in the World Championship and there are still stages that I don't remember, and when you're driving at the pace we're driving at, you

need enough information to be driving at the limit at every point of every corner – not just every corner, but every turn-in and every exit. To compensate for my lack of knowlege of stages, I have a very descriptive and complicated system – it's not really complicated, but mouthfuls. But what's good is that it's very, very rare, maybe only once on each rally, that there'll be so much information that it's hard work.'

He can no longer imagine anyone else co-driving.

'It's kind of difficult to think of having a different voice in your ear. I'm sure you'd get used to it. Sometimes I've had Steve Turvey and "Beef" [Park] sitting with me on tests and even not having a Scottish accent in your ear is strange.'

Reid certainly does not pine for the Hong Kong–Peking and acknowledges that their quarrels have usually signalled a need for compromise on both sides.

'It's not a nice environment to work in. I would say I'm not very good-tempered when I'm hungry and not very good-tempered when I'm tired. I'm a real pain in the arse to deal with when I'm tired and hungry – and I think the same is true of Richard!

'The organisation wasn't fantastic, so you were fighting with that all the time, you were fighting with the Chinese. I think one of my faults is I don't suffer fools. It can be seen as a positive, but I'm of the opinion that when you do your job professionally, the other people involved in the sport should be as professional as you are.

'I would say the relationship that Richard and I have has gone from being best mates – speak to each other every day – to barely tolerating each other, to over the last three or four years, a good, solid working relationship that errs towards friendship. I know I can rely on him and he'd be there and I think the reverse is true.

'It's an unnatural relationship that drivers and co-drivers have, because you have the stresses of doing a job and being ultra-competitive, and the relationship of, I don't know, brothers, best mates? I suppose the pressure to succeed is never there in other relationships. I think that's why I say you go through best mates, tolerance, professional, back to very trusting and good mates, but at a distance. You go through all these different phases.'

So far as Cowan and Short were con-

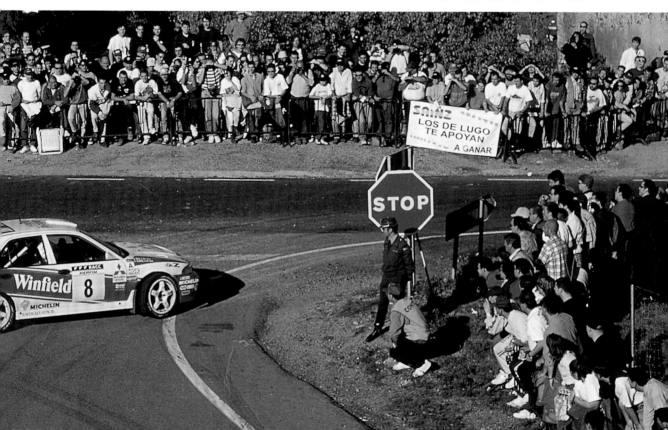

cerned, Richard's second place in the Asia-Pacific and ninth in the World Championship were more than respectable. They had ambitious plans for their junior driver for 1997. The rotation system was being scrapped and for the first time, works teams were expected to register for the World Championship and, unless they were new to the highest level, to send two full works cars to all 14 rounds. In response, Mitsubishi intended to switch its emphasis from the Far Eastern to the world stage once more. One of the official Lancers was naturally for Mäkinen, but the intention was that Burns would usually drive the other. As a sign of the team's confidence in him, it would be badged as a Carisma GT. In production terms, the Carisma and Lancer are in fact different, albeit related models. However, the Carisma is made in Europe

As the Safari has become shorter and faster, the cheetah has become a more appropriate symbol of the correct approach to winning it. To a cat lover like Richard, the attraction was obvious. (McKlein)

and a straightforward piece of form-filling with the FIA combined with a promising driver looked like a good way of boosting its image.

Richard is nothing if not image-conscious and was consequently somewhat dubious. He took a little persuading that the Carisma badge was a mark of confidence if his team-mate was driving a Lancer and he never warmed to the 1970s-style stripes that Japan devised as a livery.

More to the point, Mitsubishi had a new car, the Evo IV. There were similarities, as it used essentially the same engine as the Evo III, the same front suspension and similar principles in the four-wheel drive system, but the bodyshell and everything else was entirely new. Other teams were readying World Rally Cars – prototypes that resembled rather than mirrored production-line machinery – for the new rules, and Mitsubishi intended to meet fire with fire.

In December, Richard paid his first visit to Japan for the rally team's customary

publicity tour. Ralliart Europe management had naturally made the trip and, while Richard demonstrated the car and pressed the flesh, his bosses got an unwelcome surprise. As Mitsubishi was the only team still whole-heartedly committed to building a production model closely related to the rally car, it had spawned private, importer-run teams everywhere from Australia to Thailand, Italy and Sweden. Much the strongest of these was Ralliart Germany, whose driver, Uwe Nittel, had finished a close second in the 1996 Group N World Championship. To Ralliart Europe's dismay, it emerged that Japan proposed to offer Richard only four World Championship rounds, awarding the lion's share to Nittel.

'We felt Richard's performances were good enough to warrant a much bigger programme … Andrew and I were quite upset about that and basically thumped the table very hard, and said it was totally unacceptable and if the Japanese would care to take over the running of the rally team, then OK, we would go and let them

get on with it. And they said, "Oh no, Cowan-san, calm down, calm down!"

'But we were quite upset about it and fortunately, sense prevailed and in the end, I think Richard got seven World Championship events the following year. OK, I'm sure he would have liked more, but in the end, seven was the best we could do and we had this slightly awkward situation of Nittel being the nominated driver for some events and Richard for others.'

Gaining the experience to become a fully fledged World Championship contender in a high-speed sport would continue to be a slow process, similar in its way to studying for a degree or a professional qualification. Yet there was no other way of doing it. There were only three teams – Mitsubishi, Subaru and Ford – committed to the whole of the 1997 World

With the clutch in bad shape and time in short supply, the mechanics pushed Richard's Carisma GT in the service area during the closing stages of the 1997 Safari. (McKlein)

Championship and, in any case, the restrictions on practising stages meant that no newcomer could expect to thrash the old hands. Even Mäkinen had spent five years trying to get a team to employ him for a complete season and lack of knowledge of the roads had blunted the edge of his competitiveness as late as 1995.

Richard had found the atmosphere in Rugby very different from the outset.

'It was a lot more down to earth. There was no PR work as such. The guys are the backbone of that team. They haul themselves through a lot,' he said, referring to the mechanics. Some of this was welcome – nobody wants to become a rally driver so that he can meet more sponsors' guests,

Richard's ability to avoid punctures on the Safari borders on the uncanny, but they remain a far greater hazard in Kenya than on any other World Championship rally. (McKlein)

after all – but someone as dedicated to all aspects of the job as Richard did not always welcome the extra free time. He was concerned that Mitsubishi's *laissez faire* approach to PR was selling him short when Subaru was making an effort to promote McRae to a wider audience and that his team was doing little to raise the sport's following either. He could not help noticing that his friend, Jason Plato, the touring car racer, was kept a good deal busier by Renault. Accordingly, he paid some of his own money to enlist a journalist and PR man, Jonathan Gill, to issue press releases on his behalf. For 1997, while remaining with the Greasleys, he also did an additional deal with a new management company, IAG.

'What they want to do is try to create more of an image for the sport as well as for me, but if they can get my image up, it makes selling me a hell of a lot easier – get me seen in different circles, something

more on television, something in men's magazines, something in Sunday newspapers. Mitsubishi certainly don't do anything like that,' was his explanation of IAG's role.

At the time, Ralliart was, as Short said, very much a 'no-frills rally team' and he wondered if this was altogether the sort of thing that should be occupying Richard's mind.

In fact, Richard had time to spare. The Monte Carlo and Swedish Rallies are two of the most specialised rounds of the World Championship and while he would have loved to get a first-hand idea of what they were like, they were part of Nittel's programme and his first rally was on familiar terrain, in Kenya.

It was a highly satisfying event. Richard remembers that first Carisma as the best rally car he has ever driven and he more than justified the mechanics' efforts. When Mäkinen succumbed to an epidemic of punctures, Richard was flying the Mitsubishi flag alone and he put previous experience in Group N Subarus to good use by finishing a close second to McRae. It was the first time British drivers had claimed the top two places on a World Championship rally and it might easily have been the other way round. McRae was leading by a slim but comfortable-looking margin until he ran into electrical problems during the final leg. As the current dwindled, he resorted to switching off cooling fans and even a fuel pump in a frantic attempt to keep the Impreza running until the next service point.

Despite a niggling clutch problem, Richard therefore went on the attack, hoping the Subaru might buckle under the strain. Instead, he got a puncture and nearly lost a place to Ian Duncan's Toyota. It had been a valiant effort.

He failed to finish either of his next two rallies. Third place in Portugal slipped from his grasp thanks to gearbox failure soon after a routine replacement and he retired on the top of the Sierra Grande in Argentina, having broken the rear suspension on one of the roughest stages of the event. The rules forbade outside assis-

tance and although his mechanics were on hand to advise him, they could not help him fix the broken link.

Thereafter, he settled into a rhythm. He came fourth on the Acropolis, fourth in New Zealand, fourth in Indonesia and again in Australia and on the RAC. His gravel note driver Simon Davison mockingly suggested that Richard would go looking for a problem if there was any danger of his finishing higher, but as Davison well knew, the fourth places were not simply a noticeable improvement on most of his earlier World Championship results, but sold Richard short.

Davison is an extrovert northerner with an utter disregard for authority and is a former works driver in his own right.

Mervyn Wheeler (left) was Ralliart's doctor when Richard joined and the two have become close friends. The jacket was designed to cool the driver in unrelenting tropical heat. (McKlein)

Ralliart management had distinctly mixed feelings about him, but he had played his part in Richard's improving form. Richard's ability to pace himself and preserve the car was well established, but that would not win compressed, late-1990s World Championship rallies with just 250 stage miles. The next step was to find that extra yard of speed that the press had suggested he lacked and part of the process was to place absolute faith in his pace notes; Davison, teamed with 'Beef' Park, worked industriously to build up his driver's confidence.

Naturally, the team management also played its part. Short is

Richard was urged to believe in himself and go faster

nothing if not methodical and Richard was given a series of targets. He was never put under pressure to win, but before Argentina Short told him that he felt it was time that he set a fastest stage time on a World Championship rally. Most drivers with Richard's capabilities would have cleared that hurdle long since, but they would probably have performed a good deal more erratically and caused a good deal of extra panel damage as well. Far from being warned to behave and exercise a little self-discipline – the kind of reproach that had rung in Colin McRae's ears more than once – Richard had to be urged to believe in himself and extend himself. True enough, he clipped a rock and broke the suspension, but he had also reached the target, setting two fastest times.

It would have taken a slice of luck, but Richard might have won the next round of the World Championship, the Acropolis. He rose to second place, splitting the works Escorts of Sainz and Kankkunen for much of the event, only to break an engine mounting near the end of the second leg. It was no great surprise. Europe's most destructive World Championship rally had exacted its customary toll. Neither of the works Subarus had got that far and instead of profiting

from McRae's early departure, Mäkinen had proceeded to knock chunks out of his Lancer and therefore trailed his team-mate for much of the distance.

Once Richard had dropped back, team orders intervened. If he was not going to beat the Fords, the management reasoned that there was no point in letting him beat Mäkinen either and he was demoted to fourth at the finish. In fact, the Carisma was buckling under the strain by then, as the block had cracked, possibly as a result of the engine mounting failure.

The result barely hinted it, but Richard recalls the Acropolis as a watershed. The Lancer Evo IV was a far superior asphalt car, but in other respects it behaved much like the Evo III and was not much easier to drive. Although he had spun messily in the second leg while battling with the Fords, he felt that he had got the knack of driving a Mitsubishi for the first time.

The engineers were definitely showing an interest. Looking back on that season, Ralliart Europe's Chief Engineer, Bernard Lindauer, did not attempt to provide a scientific explanation.

As he put it, 'It just clicked'; an engineer can no more provide a driver with the key to getting the most out of a car than he can teach him to ride a bicycle, but he can help. Richard was sent to Finland that August, even though it was one of Nittel's rallies, so that he could take part in the recce and get a grasp of the terrain. Lindauer was instrumental in making sure that Richard also joined the team for its pre-rally test so that the engineers could record some data that would help programme the electronics to suit his style for 1998.

In New Zealand, Richard was the star of the show, once Colin McRae lost a commanding lead through engine failure. Richard was never in the running to repeat his 1996 triumph and victory fell to Eriksson in the end, the Swede fending off a last-ditch assault from the Fords after

As usual, there was no lack of carnage in Indonesia. Richard avoided the worst of it to make sure of fourth place. (McKlein)

Sainz hit a stray sheep and damaged the front of his Escort.

It was not Richard's fault that he wasn't trading blows with the big names. One of the Carisma's output shafts had failed soon after the start, reducing him to three-wheel drive. He had lost two minutes before getting a chance to fix it and there was nothing like enough mileage left to allow him to make up the difference. Nevertheless, he recorded five fastest times and was quickest overall in the second and third legs, finishing 1 minute 18 seconds behind the winner. When the roads dried later in the rally, running further back aided his cause because the earlier cars swept loose gravel from the surface, but he was entitled to believe that this was another rally he might have won. Richard had done everything that could be expected of him after his team-mate had reduced his car to scrap in a desperate attempt to keep up with McRae.

A couple of months later, even Colin

United in adversity, Richard discusses the position with Juha Kankkunen (centre) and Kenneth Eriksson in Indonesia. (McKlein)

was impressed. Pulling up beside his former team-mate at a time control in Indonesia, he called across, 'You must have been doing some big skids in there, Burnsie!'

Richard grinned. He had been quickest on the final stage of the first leg, 17 seconds faster than McRae, in fact, with everyone still in the rally and fighting for seconds – and as McRae was only too aware, in the most unforgiving conditions. At times, the Sumatran stages were so slippery following overnight rain that drivers resorted to snow tyres and even then, it was not a question of whether they went off the road, but how often and how badly. Burns reckoned he had slithered off 20 times in total and was none too sure why his time on Goodyear 1 had been so good.

It was definitely a rally on which discretion paid greater dividends than valour. Neither McRae nor Mäkinen went the distance, leaving older, wiser heads to divide the spoils. Sainz won from Kankkunen, with Eriksson third. If Richard had not spun on the first stage of the final leg, he reckoned he might just have made up for

a gentle start and overhauled the Subaru man, but his caution was forgiveable after his disappointingly brief appearance in 1996.

Australia was promising and frustrating in equal measure. With a day to go, he was in third place and in the thick of the battle for victory. By the end, he was a good but slightly outpaced fourth, beaten by McRae, Mäkinen and Auriol. Richard felt he had been near-enough on the limit and had not put a wheel wrong, but the others had somehow found an extra gear for the showdown in Bunnings. He was happy that he could drive at 100 per cent; the next step was to find, if only for a limited period, another 10 per cent.

The RAC posed the question with renewed urgency. On home ground, Richard was naturally in the spotlight and now possessed the confidence and the experience to be McRae's closest challenger. Two days of furious action in the forests of Wales demonstrated that he no longer had anything to fear from Sainz or Kankkunen – both former RAC winners – on home soil, but beating McRae was another matter.

He certainly ruffled the Scot's feathers. Colin had no choice but go flat out and hope that Mäkinen's ultra-reliable Mitsubishi might fail him. If Tommi scored just one point, even victory would not suffice. It was a task that McRae relished and, under the circumstances, there was no question of Richard being slowed by team orders.

The Subaru man barged into the lead from the start, only to find that he therefore had to run first the next morning, when dense fog blanketed Radnor Forest. He lost a minute and a half. Burns had hung back a little in the short first leg, realising that a lower position in the running order would give him a little more daylight in Radnor. Driving brilliantly in the fog, in only marginally better conditions, he burst into the lead. Colin had plummetted to seventh.

Initially, McRae concluded that both the rally and the championship were lost, but his anger soon took a more construc-

An early delay ruined his chances of repeating his 1996 victory, but Richard was one of the star performers in New Zealand. (McKlein)

In his second season with Mitsubishi, Richard's growing assurance and experience became apparent, even if the results did not always do him justice. (McKlein)

tive turn. He swept the visitors aside with a barrage of fastest times and drew level with Richard that night. In Hafren, he was almost half a minute faster than anyone in spite of a spin. His co-driver, Nicky Grist, admitted that he had never been driven so quickly through a forest in his life.

Richard had collected a 10-second road penalty when a rear suspension change took longer than scheduled thanks to a cross-threaded bolt, but it did not look as though it would make the difference between winning and losing. When the BBC brought the two challengers together for an interview in Builth Wells that evening, McRae sounded easy-going and confident. If there were any worries

gnawing at the back of his mind, Richard Burns evidently was not one of them. As for Richard, he sounded like the defiant little brother, protesting in the face of all the evidence that he was just as good.

His mood was understandable, partly because of McRae's turn of speed, partly because spectators had told him that they hoped he would not win, on the basis that McRae could not deprive Mäkinen of the World Championship otherwise. It was not meant personally, but Richard is a sensitive character and took it as a slight nonetheless.

He gave McRae another jolt the next morning though. It was foggy again and both of them tackled the stage in similar

An enthralling duel on the 1997 RAC suggested that Richard was becoming a true match for Colin McRae, but a puncture towards the end demoted him to a frustrated fourth. (McKlein)

conditions. Unaccountably, McRae's lights were set incorrectly and Richard profited to the tune of 17 seconds. McRae's anticipated victory no longer looked so certain. Perhaps the battle would have edged in the Subaru man's favour anyway, but it was a vile dose of luck that deprived Richard of his chance. Punctures are almost a thing of the past on most World Championship rallies, because the leading tyre makers have developed run-flat systems that allow drivers to continue at almost unabated speed.

Two stages after he had regained the lead, Richard hit a rock and the blow pinched the tyre bead. It was not a bad impact by any means, but it foiled the Michelin's defences. Instead of inflating, the foam insert popped out and the tyre deflated. Other competitors noticed the foam ring at the roadside. There was nothing for it but to swap the tyre in the conventional manner and inevitably, Richard ended up in fourth.

It surprised me a bit this year how big a step I've made

Until then, it had taken a truly exceptional performance from McRae to get the better of him and other competitors did not conceal their admiration. Indeed, at the following service point, next to a derelict factory on the edge of Resolfen, McRae walked across and clambered into the Carisma for a chat. It was a token of respect.

Mitsubishi had plenty to celebrate anyway, as a groggy, 'flu-ridden Mäkinen staggered home in sixth place to retain his world title, but Richard had emphatically proven that Ralliart was not a one-man band.

'I think the year as a whole saw him come of age. We could see that he was fast. He had fastest times and we saw that he could finish rallies. I think also it gave him quite a lot of self-belief. We saw the Richard Burns approach to rallies and that is one of consistently applying pressure, rather than being erratic – you know, sort of fastest time here and

then a disaster somewhere else. His performances were fairly even. He was pretty well always in the points,' Short commented.

Richard's growing assurance meant that he was increasingly in favour, even though the World Champion was naturally the team's priority. Mitsubishi was keen to cement a long-term relationship and Richard had been to Japan to test the forthcoming Lancer Evo V before Mäkinen.

Richard had analysed his 1997 performances in just as much detail as Short and felt that the summit was in view at last.

'There is a pattern to how I rally. I've got graphs I can show you with my stage times on, and mine and Kankkunen's are very similar in their consistency. Everyone else's are a little more erratic. I can see how my rally pans out: I don't know what's going to happen, but I know what I'm thinking, when I'm thinking it and why I'm thinking it. I don't sit and study it and worry about it – anything like that – but I can see what's going on and my rallies do normally take some kind of pattern.

'What I need to do is move the whole thing up. It surprised me a little bit this year how big a step I've made, but if you look at the rallies since New Zealand last year, there has been a gradual improvement in form and consistency as well, I would say.

'I think I've had two chances taken away from me by bad luck or whatever you want to call it, in both Greece and New Zealand this year, where I'd have been in a position to win. I'd like to think I could have won one of those two.

'If you compare my position to Colin's, then he's been fairly lucky in that after about a year of doing a bitza programme, he was banged into a full programme, so he's ahead of me there, for sure, but that's the position I want to be in next year. I'd like to win a rally next year. I know that I can win rallies. I know that it'll take time to come and I'm not rushing it. It may take time, but it will come. I don't doubt that.'

The winning feeling

The finish was a few stages off yet, but Didier Auriol had won his personal battle. The 1998 Catalonia Rally was in the palm of his hand and Toyota need not think about substituting him with Freddy Loix again. His mind had turned to other things and, noticing a clutch of British journalists, he volunteered his admiration for Richard Burns.

Richard? Good old Richard, in fourth place again? Auriol knew that results can be misleading. Burns, he pronounced, was the pick of the rising stars. After a

On his first encounter with the Monte, Richard met with just about as wide a range of conditions as the rally can provide. He passed the test with flying colours, finishing fifth. (McKlein)

decade at the top of the sport, the diminutive Frenchman knew how hard it was for a driver in Richard's position to make a

For a few hours, the gentle pace of rural life is jolted into a blur of frenetic action. Kenyan villagers take shelter to watch Richard on his way to a momentous Safari victory. (McKlein)

lasting impact. It was only his second attempt at Catalonia and, as it happened, the Lancer Evo V was not quite living up to expectations on its first appearance. But Richard's results that year had gone well beyond confirming 1997's favourable impression. He had joined the elite.

When Auriol had made his first World

Championship forays, making a good impression on a limited number of events had been easier. On most rallies, there were to all intents and purposes no recce restrictions. Practising stages in what amounted to a rally car lacking only the numbers on the doors was widely condoned. Seasoned drivers often spent weeks checking the route and refining their notes, and for newcomers it was essential. The rules of engagement had changed utterly in the 1990s. If drivers were to contest 13 or 14 World Championship rallies in a year, it was generally accepted that they would have to spend less time practising and the teams

liked the idea of using slower, cheaper recce cars in any case. By 1998, three or four runs per stage were the maximum permitted, which presented a considerable advantage to drivers who had attempted the rally and the same stages in the past. The newcomer was in much the same predicament as a racing driver would be if he went to a strange circuit, did three or four exploratory laps in a fast road car, then climbed into a Formula 1 car for a grand prix.

That was the challenge Richard had faced on the Monte Carlo and Swedish rallies. On the Monte, it was not just a matter of learning the stages, but learning the tyre permutations. For the first time in his life, he was contesting a rally on studded tyres and trying to assess a bewilder-

Richard and Robert had joined a select band: prior to their triumph on the 1998 Safari, only two British drivers had won World Championship rallies. (McKlein)

ing array of different types for a rally that often provides fresh snow, dry asphalt and everything in between. Works teams routinely have nearly a dozen tyre permutations to consider. Fifth place was therefore highly satisfying from a personal point of view as well as the team's.

Fifteenth on his first Swedish was less striking, yet it did not conceal his promise either. Inevitably, he had slithered into a snowbank and thrown away several minutes digging his way out. Most novices do. If he had been lucky, he would have lost two minutes. If he had been particularly unlucky, he could have lost 25. As it was, he dropped nine, but as early as the second stage. Even though he would not score World Championship points, there was still much to learn on his first true snow rally.

By the next morning, Mäkinen was taking a keen interest in his team-mate's times, which was a remarkable state of affairs considering that he was on his way

to his second Swedish victory and knew the rally almost as well as the locals. Richard was setting an eyecatching pace. He was quickest on two stages and his colleague concluded that the tyres must be making the difference. That was the last Richard saw of the Michelin GEs. He had to be content with proving a point.

When it came to the Safari Richard was in no sense a novice and any mistakes would have been much harder to forgive. As the last day unfolded, that knowledge was preying on his mind. He had made a mistake and his fate was in the hands of his mechanics. Even old Safari hands such as Kankkunen had not realised that the World Championship's last road race was fought out at such a ferocious pace and that it was no longer a trial of strength and restraint. Richard had judged it to perfection, he had been amongst the leaders from the start and, when Mäkinen and both works Subarus succumbed to engine failures for one reason or another (in

Tommi's case, he had triggered it by smashing an engine mounting), he swept into a clear lead.

A 10-minute margin over the works Escorts of Vatanen and Kankkunen was not much by Safari standards. If Richard kept his nerve, he would win, but the Ford men were close enough to exert pressure and Richard needed a good start to the final leg to snuff out the Finnish counterattack at once. He had no sooner stepped up the pace than he clouted a rock and damaged the sump.

The rock had not been there when the same section had been used on the first day. The roads had deteriorated still further – which meant that something similar might happen again – but the immediate problem was that the sump had to be replaced at once to stem the oil leak. The

Kenya provides abundant opportunities to relax as well. Richard is one of the many visitors to have combined the Safari with a holiday. (McKlein)

knowledge that the engine was otherwise in good health was little consolation: 20 minutes were permitted for service, a sump change was expected to take a minimum of 25 and that would not only gnaw into his lead – perhaps devour it altogether – but allow Vatanen to go first on the road. He would then have a dust-free run and Mitsubishi would have lost the initiative. No wonder Richard was chewing his fingers nervously. No wonder Cowan – a long-distance expert with a distinguished Safari record of his own – observed that the Safari is won and lost in service.

The mechanics surpassed themselves. The sump was replaced in 22 frantic minutes. With three-minute intervals between cars, Richard was still first on the road and still in the lead.

Despite roads that invited an error and the realisation that Vatanen and Kankkunen had been in this position dozens of times, there were no more slips,

An occasional presence but a constant influence, David Williams (right), has played an essential role in nurturing Richard's career. (McKlein)

no chance for the Escort men to get on terms. Richard negotiated all the hazards and pushed every nagging uncertainty to the back of his mind. After a short final section around the Ngong horse racing track – a Sunday drive compared with the car-eating sections in the bush – the car-crazed youth who had stacked supermarket shelves and rallied in borrowed cars became a World Championship rally winner at last.

After so many hours of relentless pressure, eloquence was perhaps too much to expect.

'I wanted to win it, but there are a lot of variables in this rally. I had the experience to do it, the car to do it and the mechanics have been fantastic,' he said as he shook hands with every member of the team. It had been a physically and emotionally draining week.

'You're actually making me cry. I don't like crying,' said a delighted Cowan.

'You're crying for the right reason,' the winner responded.

His rivals saluted an outstanding performance.

'Fantastic: good drive. He has been doing well a long time and he deserved this. He drove a constant speed all rally. Ten out of ten,' Kankkunen said. Coming from someone who has won three Safaris, that was praise indeed.

'It's very special. To win any Safari is special; having been there and competed, I know how difficult it is and how it can kick back when you think you're doing all right, but to have two young guys who we've had for three years, it's better. They've won it from the front – and one of the most difficult rallies in the world,' said Cowan, after he'd wiped his eyes.

It is an auspicious occasion when any driver wins his first World Championship rally. When the driver is only the third Briton to do so, when the rally in question is the Safari and when he's driving for what is essentially a British team, it has to be celebrated with some abandon and, naturally, Ralliart's celebrations focused on the hotel swimming pool in Nairobi. Several members of the team were

reminded of the occasion every time they looked in the mirror. Everyone who had a moustache, including the Team Manager, Phil Short, had had it shaved off – whether they volunteered or not.

Winning the Safari was a watershed, but Richard knew that there was unfinished business.

'I think there's still a duck to break so far as a sprint event is concerned,' he reflected.

He was quite right, but he was being regarded in a new light before that duck was broken. In the spring, Prodrive made contact. Regardless of whether McRae signed again or moved to Ford – and the betting was that he would move – Subaru wanted Burns back.

The Safari was followed by a series of

Concentration is the key: at the wheel of his Carisma GT, Richard is entirely dedicated to the task in hand. (McKlein)

less memorable results. The Evo V had more power, a faster computer (almost as important as a bigger turbo or an extra gear) and wider-track suspension, but it took a while to get the most out of it. In the meantime, Richard made do with fourth in Argentina as well as Catalonia.

Corsica was a struggle. It is widely regarded as the most demanding asphalt rally of all and Short had advised him that he would do well to score points. He was on the fringe of the top six when he slid wide on the last corner of a stage and smashed the suspension against a kerb, retiring at the opposite end of the village.

Characteristically, Richard found some cause for satisfaction, pointing out that he had been quickest Michelin runner on several stages.

On the Acropolis, he learnt the hard way that taking the lead is not necessarily worth anything more than tomorrow's headlines. Running first on the road over dirt tracks that were as dry as tinder ensured that he acted as gravel plough and he had much less grip than his pursuers. He was soon overhauled and his efforts to catch up were rewarded with broken suspension.

Ninth place meant that there were no points in New Zealand either, yet with a following wind, he might have snatched another win. He was in touch with the dominant Toyotas as the final leg began, only to tip the car gently on to its roof. The damage was minimal, but it took an age to find some spectators and the crew could not right almost a ton and a half of Carisma alone.

If there is a loose-surface equivalent of Corsica, it is the Rally Finland, frequently known by its old name, as the 1000 Lakes. The two rallies could not be more different in character, as the Finnish stages are considerably faster and best known for the hundreds of jumps that launch cars into the air for yards at a time. The similarities are that knowing the road and the right line is crucial, that the locals are extremely hard to beat and that first-timers risk being eaten alive.

Richard was not eaten alive. He loves fast stages and demonstrated the fact by finishing fifth, then the best ever result for a British driver – one place better than Paddy Hopkirk and Russell Brookes had managed in 1965 and 1982 respectively. It was a striking performance and not just because so few British drivers have done well in Finland. It had also become McRae's bogey rally and although he was quicker at first, the

Richard's fortunes veered constantly on the 1998 Rally Australia. A spell in the lead was followed by two rolls, the second within an hour of the finish when neck and neck for the lead. (McKlein)

Subaru man soon ran wide and broke the suspension.

Mäkinen is near-unbeatable in Finland, but elsewhere Richard could no longer be dismissed as the cautious, overshadowed understudy.

'I've proven on a few occasions that I can have the measure of Tommi. Of course, there are going to be places where he's going to be quicker, because of his experience, but it's been nice not to be the one who's always second into *parc ferme* in the morning: it means you get the front seat on the lift on the way there!' he said.

Status mattered and Richard was chafing increasingly at Ralliart. He had been nurtured carefully and he expressed his gratitude to Cowan and Short for allowing him to develop at his own pace, but he had become impatient at being part of Tommi's team. There were all kinds of little grievances, from the regular presence of Mäkinen's noisy entourage in the motorhome to the fact that while the World Champion, along with most of the top drivers, flew first class, Richard and Robert were in business class. Nor was he prepared to overlook being on the same salary as he was when he joined Mitsubishi.

He wanted more support in other ways too, from advice on fitness to a more positive attitude to promotion and sponsorship. Above all, he wanted to be in a position in which he was a number one driver and the question of dropping behind Mäkinen did not arise.

There was room for negotiation with Ralliart on some of these points, but Prodrive's offer was skilfully framed. For the first time in his life, Richard was being offered the prospect of becoming a millionaire.

'Obviously, we would have liked to have hung on to him. We knew that we had Tommi for another year, but our view was longer term and we were looking to have a replacement within the team should

> ## He might be number one now but he'd have to really fight for it

Mäkinen go elsewhere at the end of '99,' Short explained.

'But we had a meeting with Richard and Mike Greasley in the middle of the year and they told us what was on offer so far as Prodrive was concerned. It was a very good offer, in two ways: financially, obviously it was much stronger than Richard was getting with us, but also, he would no longer be a number-two driver. In the middle of the year Andrew and I went to Japan and put the case for retaining Richard, but basically, they told us we cannot afford Mäkinen and Burns if that is the rate.

'I think even if we had been able to match the Prodrive money, Richard would have found it difficult to remain with us, because he would effectively have still been number two. OK, it wasn't formalised in such a way, but the set-up of the team was such that he would find it hard to foresee a situation like happened with Ferrari last year of him suddenly having the number-one status. Obviously, if Tommi had a bad year and Richard had a good year, that would certainly have been the case, but the chance to be free of such restrictions was obviously as attractive to Richard as it was to Irvine at the end of last year. We fully understood his point of view and resigned ourselves to losing him.'

The discussions were not always conducted in quite such a cordial manner. It was put to Richard that he was being ungrateful and that taking off at the first opportunity did not repay the debt he owed Mitsubishi.

Greasley retorted that loyalty was a two-way process.

'I had to point out to Andrew that if you put a dummy in the shop window, someone will want to buy it eventually. He took the point, as did Richard!'

The deal was announced in September, a matter of weeks after McRae's departure to Ford was confirmed. Richard would rejoin Subaru in 1999 for three years, as team-mate to the genial and gentle Belgian, Bruno Thiry. Richard was the number-one driver, the man who would get the lion's share of the attention, the pick of the tyres and any seat he wanted in the minibus on the way to *parc ferme*. At least, he was until Prodrive announced that it was also signing Kankkunen.

The news took Richard completely unawares. There had been no suggestion that Subaru intended to run a three-car team, far less that it would hire a four-times World Champion as the extra driver. Kankkunen was not noted for his speed on asphalt, but his record on any other rally spoke for itself and, like most successful Finnish sportsmen, he did not have a reputation for taking prisoners. He was 39 at the time and it would be fair to say that his best years as a driver were behind him, but he was still very definitely a carnivore. Richard was being offered an opportunity to be number one that had not been on the table at Ralliart, but he was still going to have to fight for it.

In the meantime, there was unfinished business at Mitsubishi. Mäkinen had fought back brilliantly after a distinctly uneven start to the season and a late surge had carried him to the brink of his third championship. Ralliart had played its full part. Lindauer had finally prevailed upon Japan to re-programme the differentials so that they locked under braking and the Lancer became an even more formidable car as a result. Mäkinen responded with superb victories in Sanremo and Australia, whereas Richard experienced very different fortunes.

He would have been in the points on his first attempt at the Italian rally if it was not for an electrical problem near the end that dropped him to seventh. In contrast, a strong start propelled him into the lead

The rivalry is keen, but entirely without rancour. Richard's 1998 season culminated in a dramatic battle with Colin McRae for the Rally of Great Britain. (McKlein)

in Australia. It was a mixed blessing. As in Greece, running first meant that he was the gravel plough and was sure to lose time as a result. There was no sense in being cautious: better to go in search of that extra 10 per cent when he was certain to lose the lead anyway. In the event, he hastened the process by rolling, but that put him in a strong position for the final leg, another nerve-jangling confrontation in Bunnings. Fourth on the road, he was soon reeling in Mäkinen and Sainz hand over fist and, with two stages to run, five seconds covered the top four, with McRae narrowly in the lead.

Red is the colour: Richard and Mitsubishi celebrate his 1998 win on the Rally of Great Britain and a clean sweep for the team: Richard's triumph clinched the manufacturers' world title, while Tommi Mäkinen retained the drivers' crown. (McKlein)

There was not much scope for team orders with a Ford and a Subaru very much in contention and Richard redoubled the attack. He was rewarded with another roll for his pains – a much more substantial one this time – forcing him to retire.

A few days later, he rolled again in a test for the 1998 Rally of Great Britain (the new name for the RAC Rally). When pushed, he will throw those three excursions back in the interviewer's face, to nail the slur that he is squeamish about damaging cars. Richard's development path has been unconventional. It has plotted neatly on a graph – but he likes it to be known that he is a red-blooded rally driver nonetheless, as if the question were still in doubt.

The idea that he might win the Rally of Great Britain was no longer fanciful,

but not universally accepted either. Rather than interview the automatic favourite, McRae, *Motoring News* brought both the Lanark man and his Subaru replacement together for lunch and a joint interview in Sanremo. Richard no longer sounded like the little brother when he quietly asserted that he could win. The McRae camp remained a touch dismissive.

Burns had stamped his views on the occasion in another way besides, refusing to wear an England rugby shirt for the photos. With some heat, he rejected it as a misguided publicity stunt. It had taken a long time to find two British rally drivers with a real chance of World Championship success and he saw no reason to create an artificial, English–Scottish divide. He might have added that his co-driver is Scottish and McRae's, Nicky

Grist, is Welsh. The challengers, he pointed out, were all British.

In fact, there was another McRae to consider. It had taken Alister a while longer to get his hands on a full-time World Championship drive, but his potential could no longer be overlooked and Prodrive offered him the second of its three Imprezas for the home event.

Alister admitted that it would take him a few miles to get the hang of the car and although he shared the lead with his older brother after the first stage around Cheltenham Racecourse, he could not be expected to sustain that

Richard meets the World Land Speed Record holder, Andy Green. The two disciplines are not as far apart as they might seem, as a spell at a rally school was part of Green's training for the record attempt. (McKlein)

sort of form as the pace increased.

The battle for supremacy remained an all-British affair. Mäkinen crashed heavily on the fifth stage at Millbrook when he hit a patch of oil left by a Hillman Imp contesting the Historic rally and, after that, Sainz needed only fourth to be certain of the title.

Burns and McRae were competing solely for pride, but if anything that made the contest fiercer still. Neither had anything to lose and both had a point to prove. Both knew that they would be judged at home on this one rally. Only a sliver of the audience would consider the thousands of miles covered in the previous 12 events.

It was a much more finely balanced contest than it had been in 1997. When the rally entered the forests on the second morning, it was foggy again in Radnor and Richard was quickest once more, but this time McRae was barely a second behind; first blood to the pretender nevertheless.

It's the best way to leave – how many ups can you get?

Richard was quickest again on the next stage, Myherin, albeit by just 3/10ths of a second and he moved into the lead when Colin spun on a horribly slimy test in Tywi. Fired up, the Impreza man responded with consecutive fastest times in Esgair Dafydd, Crychan and Cefn to regain the lead. The battle looked as though it was turning slowly but inexorably in his favour, but then the Subaru's engine fell sick. They are tough and regularly take enormous punishment, but this one was beyond redemption. It expired in a cloud of smoke and steam at the service area in Builth Wells.

McRae and Grist apart, no one was more disappointed than Richard. He had craved an RAC victory, of course, but he wanted above all to do so in a straight fight with McRae. The duel had carried him well clear of the pursuit, which was led by Alister in the surviving Subaru and when he rolled in fog early the next morning, Richard was free to cruise through the Glamorgan forests.

Perhaps it was not exactly a cruise though. There were niggling problems with the car – a jammed wheel nut and an electronic gremlin in the transmission that upset the handling, but he continued to set fastest times at will, smashing stage record after stage record. Short could only shake his head in wonder, confident nevertheless that his driver knew what he was doing. By the time Richard emerged from the last stage at Margam, victory had become a formality.

'I'm leaving the team. It's the best way to go. How many ups can you get? I first did this rally in 1990 and I never dreamt I'd be here today,' the victor said.

It was such an accomplished, assured performance that it was slightly overshadowed by the events of the last stage. Sainz's Toyota blew its engine with the flying finish in sight and Mäkinen, who had been holed up in Cheltenham for two days, discovered to his astonishment that he was World Champion after all. It was a memorable finale: Mäkinen had become the first man to win the World Rally Championship three times running, while Luis Moya, Sainz's co-driver, had flung his crash helmet through the Corolla's rear window with rage and grief.

Thanks to Richard, Mitsubishi had scored its fourth consecutive win and claimed the World Championship for Manufacturers for the first time. For all Mäkinen's brilliance, that would have been impossible without an exceptionally capable team-mate. At the celebrations that night, Richard was far from forgotten. The mechanics who had gloomily fixed a succession of crumpled cars almost three years before had turned into some of his strongest supporters.

Richard had his sprint victory. He had joined Colin McRae and Roger Clark as only the third British driver to have won the RAC Rally since 1960. He had reminded the world that there is more than one British rallyman worth the name. All the figures on the graph looked good.

chapter seven

Reap what you sow

In his Mitsubishi years, there were times when Richard devoutly wished he was still driving a Subaru. When the opportunity arrived at last to revert, he soon came to appreciate that the Carisma had not been so bad after all. He was far too professional to detail the Impreza's failings in public, but neither the engine, the shock absorbers nor the tyres met with his approval during initial tests. His first few rallies on his return to the Banbury team were neither fruitful nor auspicious.

On the first event of the season, the Monte, he slid off for over two minutes on the atrociously slippery first stage, then displayed an uncanny knack for picking the wrong tyres in changeable conditions. It left him very firmly at the tail end of Subaru's trio, with no points, while his old team-mate Mäkinen pocketed another win. The Swedish event was not much better, as Pirelli's studded tyres were still no match for Michelin's and the works Imprezas consequently never stood a chance.

It was nevertheless a very important rally indeed for Richard and there was an unusual degree of satisfaction to be derived from coming fifth. He was embroiled in the fiercest, most-prolonged battle of the event, waged without quarter against his new team-mate, Juha Kankkunen. If Burns was going to earn number one status, losing to the four-times World Champion was unthinkable, even in conditions that were much more familiar to a farmer's son from central Finland than a computer expert's boy from Britain's Home Counties. To Kankkunen's ill-disguised chagrin, Richard made his point, by 5.1 seconds.

The Safari was familiar ground for both of them and on past form, more profitable for Subaru as well. Richard forced his way into the lead and had just begun to gain the upper hand when a bolt failed and the suspension collapsed. If anything, Portugal was more depressing still. True, he finished fourth, but Colin McRae won for the second time running; so much for the Scot languishing in the doldrums while his new Ford fell apart and Richard demonstrated he was more than capable of filling his shoes at Subaru.

No-one had regarded Richard as a likely World Champion at the beginning of the 1999 season, on the basis that there was a number of rallies he did not yet know sufficiently well, but he had hoped for a good deal more than a meagre haul of five points from his first four rallies. He

He drove his heart out for very little reward – or recognition

was driving his heart out for very little reward and, to his irritation, for practically no recognition either, as a couple of journalists were told in plain language.

Pirelli had begun to lag behind Michelin on dry asphalt as well and the Subarus were mauled again in Catalonia and Corsica. Prodrive's Chairman Richards suggested that McRae had probably masked Pirelli's declining competitiveness, a remark that predictably needled Burns. The implication was clear enough.

'I was probably the most despondent in Portugal. In Monte Carlo and Sweden, it was fairly easily attributable. In Portugal, I could set fastest times, but I couldn't keep doing it without going off the road; I was off the road a lot on that rally. I wasn't taken aback, but I was frustrated, because it seemed that every time we made a little bit of a move forward, then everyone else

Although leaving Mitsubishi gave Richard a free hand to compete against Tommi Mäkinen head on, the Finn still led the 1999 World Championship from start to finish. (McKlein)

went a bit further and especially with tyres. Sometimes Pirelli are a little bit guilty of saying, "We've made an improvement," and you have to say, "It's not it. We need more." It's a lot of perseverance from me and Prodrive.

'I was frustrated that we didn't have the points, that was the thing. I drove some of my best rallies at the beginning of that year. I beat Juha on my second ever visit to Sweden. I beat everyone in the team on Tarmac – OK, Juha, fair enough, but I've beaten Bruno [Thiry] in Corsica and in Spain. I was doing everything I could,' Richard commented.

The press had latched on to the fact that Subaru, of all teams, had gone almost 12 months without a win. There were even suggestions, firmly denied by Prodrive and Subaru Tecnica International in Japan, that the rally programme might be wound up. In the prevailing atmosphere, the Rally of Argentina was not simply a triumph, but a godsend. Although they were never far ahead of their rivals, the Imprezas were in a class of their own and collected first and second

entirely on merit. Yet Richard left Argentina with a distinctly bitter taste. The rally had looked to be his for the taking, despite an electronic problem with Prodrive's new semi-automatic gearbox which cost him 10 seconds in penalties at a time control. He was in the lead for most of the way and, while there was no chance of settling into a cruise when Auriol's Toyota was within range, the instructions to the Subaru drivers were unambiguous: they were to take no risks and to hold station. Indeed, Kankkunen was resigned to his fate. As he said, he had been on the receiving end of team orders often enough.

But Richard became vulnerable as the finish neared, because he was running first on the road. As the stages had dried, he was therefore sweeping a thin layer of gravel and losing grip, while improving the surface for his rivals. It wasn't costing much time, but it gave Kankkunen the chance to steal closer and eventually, the temptation was too great: the older man had not won a World Championship rally in five years, he knew that the FIA's offi-

cial disapproval of team orders would make it hard for Prodrive to force him to take extra penalties and sacrifice a victory achieved on the road, and he accordingly 'misinterpreted' the signal held out to him by a team member on the last stage, claiming that he thought he was being told to speed up rather than slow down.

In the confusion, Richard did not even know that he had been beaten at the post, by all of 2.4 seconds, until the author told him. A mixture of disbelief and rage had formed across the crew's features as Robert Reid slammed the car door and an animated conversation began. By the time Kankkunen reached the final service point, Prodrive was putting a brave face on this unexpected turn of events. After all, it made no difference to Subaru's points score on the rally. Richard's turn would come, was the breezy official line.

Richard could not brush it aside so eas-

Catalonia attracts some of the biggest crowds of the season. Richard provided his share of the entertainment, but not much of a result, tyre problems restricting him to fifth. (McKlein)

Victory at last! Richard absorbed intense pressure on the Acropolis to score his first win for Subaru at World Championship level. (McKlein)

ily. Worst of all, complaining that the gravel had offered Kankkunen his chance and pointing out that he would have won but for his gearbox-induced penalty were apt to make him sound as though he could not look after himself when the gloves came off.

Kankkunen insisted that Auriol had been too close to allow anyone to slow down and that he was the quicker in the dash for the line, pure and simple. To Richard, his team-mate had broken his word. Rivalry now bordered on antipathy.

Under the circumstances, the Acropolis, three weeks later, was inevitably seen as a chance to settle scores as much as to score points, no matter how insistently Richard claimed that it wasn't. He stated he had put Argentina out of his mind within hours and revenge was not a useful emotion when driving rally cars. He got his revenge nevertheless.

Subaru generally does well in Greece

and it was no great surprise to find Richard in the lead as the first leg drew to a close, with a pack of drivers jostling in his wake. He then did something exceptionally bold: he deliberately booked into a time control late, incurred 40 seconds of penalties and dropped to fourth.

Well aware that he had surrendered chunks of time the year previously, he had decided that running first on the road in dry conditions would be too much of a handicap. Rather than be 'crucified' once again, as Richards put it, he judged that he could exploit tracks comparatively free of gravel and regain the deficit. Most World Championship rallies are decided by less than 40 seconds; it would have been intensely embarrassing had it gone wrong, but Burns's judgement was immediately vindicated. It took him only two stages to regain the lead, but just when he

Noted, sorted: Richard's pace notes are amongst the most detailed of any top rally driver's. Robert Reid handles the intricate process of getting the information on paper and relaying it to his driver with unflustered efficiency. (McKlein)

seemed poised to pull away, an electronic fault shut down the semi-automatic gearbox not once, but twice in water crossings.

Appropriately, Finland's round of the World Championship used to be known as the 1000 Lakes. Finishing second was one of the highlights of Richard's 1999 season. (McKlein)

He lost around half a minute in total and temporarily ceded the upper hand to Mäkinen. Nonetheless, he was soon back in front and when McRae's gearbox expired later that afternoon, his advantage began to look comfortable, if not impregnable.

Although the last leg was shorter, the

stages near the rally's base in Agii Theodori were exceptionally rough and both Sainz and Mäkinen were close enough to fancy their chances of winning. Again, Richard's tactics were impeccable. At his suggestion, one of Prodrive's gravel note crews went out shortly after dawn to roll the worst of the boulders out of the

way on the morning's first stage. He paced himself a little through the opening miles, eased the Subaru through the ford, then went on the attack. He was fastest and the car was still in good shape, whereas both of his most dangerous adversaries hobbled out with suspension trouble.

It was an unqualified triumph, absolute

proof that he had the talent and the temperament to win against any opposition. The celebrations continued well into the night. Looking back over the first half of the season, Richard could draw some satisfaction not just from the marked improvement in Subaru's fortunes, but from his part in the process.

'In a way, I was enjoying it, because I was learning also how far I could push and then when it came to the end of the year, I was driving just the same, but I was just driving a better car, because of the things that had been developed, based on what we'd said. A lot of it was dampers. A lot of it was basically because they'd been running with Colin and Piero Liatti, who were both leaving and therefore had no interest in making the car good for the rest of the year.

Richard relaxes with friends, near Oxford. Unlike many top drivers, he has rejected being a tax exile in favour of maintaining his private life. (McKlein)

'It was a new car anyway, so Prodrive were really keen to try loads of new stuff with us, because we'd be open to ideas and we didn't have anything pre-set in our minds. Colin had been there for however many years, seven years, and there are going to be some things that if you've never driven another car you're not going to know can be done. And I knew what was good in the Mitsubishi and I knew what wasn't good.'

The Acropolis result notwithstanding, Prodrive shared Williams's view that lack of self-confidence rather than ability had been Richard's problem.

'He needs support and he needs to be loved by a team. He likes the team around him, like Heinz-Harald Frentzen. He's not a hard person, he's not a brash person. He drives through skill and delicacy. If you believe in Richard, he'll go faster and faster and faster,' is how Williams puts it. Prodrive management was prepared to lavish some love on its lead driver and Richard had already begun to assemble a

group centred on him, just as he had seen Mäkinen create a Finnish cell within Ralliart. The key figures included his engineer, Simon Cole, the gravel note crew, Robbie Head and Steve Turvey, and the doctor whom he had befriended at Mitsubishi, Mervyn Wheeler.

But Prodrive felt that a little more assertiveness on the driver's part was required as well. In particular, he needed to believe that he was no longer in Colin McRae's shadow. The team therefore set up a confrontation. The occasion was the Goodwood Festival of Speed – a well-attended and well-publicised attraction for motorsport fans in southern Britain, but with nothing more than pride at stake and no great distance to cover. The hill-climb was one of the main attractions and it included a rally car class, for which Burns and McRae were entered in their usual cars.

Prodrive hyped the occasion for all it was worth. There was talk of a special Impreza being prepared for the show-

down and, sure enough, there were some new parts for practice, but Richards insisted that for the timed runs, the car was in the same trim as it had been in Corsica. Burns was an emphatic and very public winner.

'If someone tells you long enough, long enough and just keeps repeating it to you, "Colin's a superstar and you're the next generation. You might be that one day," you might not want to accept it, but it becomes ingrained in you. You have to break that barrier and say, "No, you are the equal any day of the week and you must take up that challenge". We set a few milestones during the year to try and identify that and I think now that ghost is gone,' Richards reflected with satisfaction.

It was part of the process of convincing

Richard discusses car settings with his engineer, Simon Cole (left) and the team director, David Lapworth. The relationship between the three men is a crucial element in the team's fortunes. (McKlein)

Burns that he was a leader. Richards was prepared to imply not merely that McRae had disguised some of Pirelli's asphalt shortcomings, but to comment that his

Richard was frequently the pacesetter in the second half of the season and never lower than second when he finished. (McKlein)

new signing was 'well in credit' when it came to damaging cars. He liked the fact that Richard is a meticulous, even calculating driver; he compared him to the formidable German double World Champion Walter Röhrl, a man to whom driving was as much an intellectual as a physical process. But he also felt that

Richard needed to extend himself and take command.

'Teams need leaders and the most obvious person to lead a team is the number one driver. They're the ones that influence the whole way that a team believes in itself and it's only through his actions and the role that he takes that everything else follows. I think for Richard, very much because he was the third driver in our team last time around, and very much at Mitsubishi he was treated as the number two, it was onerous as much as it was an acknowledgement of his abilities. In the last few months, he has made enormous demonstrations of his maturity, his com-

Limited chances for service mean that the driver's mechanical skills matter more than ever, especially on the rougher events. Richard has worked hard on increasing his practical knowledge of the Impreza. (McKlein)

mitment to the team as much as their commitment to him and those things don't go unnoticed. I'll be quite blunt: he came to the team with – there's a slight aloofness about him, if you like. He's not easy to get close to. Those barriers have been broken now,' Richards concluded that autumn.

For a young man who becomes very wealthy very fast, it can be hard to distinguish friends from hangers-on who are more interested in a slice of the celebrity and the money. That may account in part for the 'aloofness' that Richards identified. In fact, there was evidence that Richard was feeling more comfortable with his circumstances in his private as well as his public life.

Hitherto, he could not be accused of spending money like a playboy sportsman. He had had a few motorbikes – a Triumph T595, then a Buell – and a jet ski, but he had lived in a rented house near Oxford

with his friend Colin McMaster. By early 1999, he felt able to buy a house nearby for the first time, moving in with his then girl-friend Saffron Small, and to indulge himself a little more, buying a 1969 Camaro and later on, a Porsche GT3.

A Monaco address appealed, but he initially took the unusual decision not to become a tax exile. Escaping tax for a time would be no substitute for a gypsy existence remote from friends and family, he decided. At home, Richard was perfectly comfortable slouched on a sofa, watching *The Simpsons*, free to cruise into Oxford or London. The environment mattered. Saffron, a reticent but self-possessed woman nine years his junior, was only too aware that he was rarely at home for more than a week, and at the end of 2000 the constant travel and rocketing income prompted a change of heart. Despite hav-

For generations, non-Nordic drivers avoided Finland like the plague, reasoning that they didn't stand a chance. Second place in 1999, at only his second attempt, was an outstanding feat. Richard (seen with, from the left, his co-driver Robert Reid and the victors, Juha Repo and Juha Kankkunen) knew it was a moment to savour. (McKlein)

ing bought an attractive house in the Cotswolds, Richard decided to base himself in Andorra. The financial logic of being one of the elite few earning more than £1,000,000 per year had become inescapable.

'Even when he's at home, he doesn't have time off as such. He's always training and there's always someone on the 'phone asking him about the rally or the car. So no, he doesn't switch off. Even when we were on holiday, he still was constantly on the 'phone, making sure that everything was OK, and people would 'phone him.

'He didn't talk about himself at all when we first met. He just kept asking questions about me. I said, "Right, I'm going to have to ask you something about you, because you know everything about me." I said, "What do you do?"

'He was ever so cagey and he was like, "I'm a sports person". I went, "Right, would you like to tell me a bit more?"

'And he was like, "No, that's it". So I had to prise out of him what he did, I had to guess whether he was a footballer, whether it involved a gun or a ball or a racket. He finally admitted that he was a rally driver and I was kind of a bit disappointed, to be honest, because I'd been involved with a couple of drivers before and it was always a nightmare, and I swore blind that I would never get involved with a driver. But he made me laugh and he was just so funny and I just felt myself warming to him, so I thought, "Well, I'll continue to give it a chance".'

Saffron made occasional appearances on rallies and was in Greece to witness Richard's Acropolis victory, but she probably did the right thing in missing New Zealand. The gearbox failed in the first leg, when Richard was the nearest challenger to Mäkinen and McRae. Another gearbox failure sidelined him at Sanremo, but these were the only real setbacks in the second half of the season. Richard was

Richard was now ready for his first serious title bid

the runner-up in Finland, just nine seconds behind Kankkunen, neck and neck with Auriol for the China Rally until he guessed wrongly on tyre choice during the final leg, which forced him to settle for second, and then a convincing winner in Australia and Britain, facing down Sainz on the former and Kankkunen back at home.

Predictably, the RAC – as the fans still call it – was portrayed as a motorised grudge match between Richard and Colin McRae. Burns did nothing to lower the temperature with some incautious remarks to the press and McRae was moved to comment that if Richards had his way, the drivers would swap driving gloves for boxing gloves.

In the event, McRae proved unusually vulnerable to the needle and the added pressure of five months without a finish. This was nothing like the battles the two had waged in 1997 and 1998. The Focus was never on the pace and Richard would have won almost as he pleased even if McRae hadn't crashed. It is never quite that easy and he had had to contend with some particularly slippery forests in South Wales, to say nothing of a heart-stopping, sixth-gear moment when he nearly threw away a comfortable lead in the second leg.

These are occupational hazards to the rally driver. He didn't crash. Instead, he had finished second in the World Championship to Mäkinen and, if the car had run a little better on Tarmac and there had been less gearbox trouble, he might even have found the eight points between him and the title.

Perhaps his most impressive performance was in Finland. Finishing second at the second attempt, on such fast roads so well known to his main opponents, was little short of astonishing. There had been nothing comfortable about Kankkunen's victory and, while he was able to return the favour and exert some pressure in Britain, he was a good deal further behind at the finish. Richard had more than fulfilled expectations. He was ready for his first serious title bid.

chapter eight

In the points, but out of luck

By May 2000, it was no longer a question of whether Richard would become World Champion, but when. That, at least, was the way it seemed as he won three times in four rallies and piled up a 14-point lead before the season was even halfway through. His confidence had soared to the extent that by the summer he was driving on to the start ramp expecting to win.

Growing experience and confidence undeniably played their part, but Richard gladly admitted that Subaru's new car, the Impreza P2000, deserved its share of the credit. Kept under cover until the Rally of Portugal to make sure that it was battle-ready, it looked near-identical to the Anglo-Japanese team's first-generation World Rally Cars, but it had been the subject of an extensive re-design beneath the skin, and the designers reckoned that it was 80 per cent new. There was nothing overtly radical about it, as it retained the WRC99's flat-four engine and semi-auto-

The Swedish is one of Richard's favourite rallies, but tyre trouble ensured that he spent most of the 2000 event out of the limelight. (McKlein)

matic gearbox as well as a good many of its body panels, but Prodrive had put a massive effort into re-examining and refining almost everything else. Wherever possible, mass had been lowered and moved within the wheelbase, the idea being to lower the centre of gravity and to reduce the polar moment of inertia. That was not something that had greatly concerned people designing rally cars when Richard started competing in Sunbeams and Escorts, but it was a contributory factor in making the car change direction more quickly. The engineers had brought a racing-style approach to rally car design, applying a remorseless attention to detail to improving grip and traction when the rules were deliberately framed to head off radical developments in many other areas. The new car featured everything from lighter suspension struts to a relocated alternator, again with the idea of lowering or saving weight.

The fact that Prodrive had adopted such a policy was a testament to Richard's

Burns has rarely had a bad Safari and the 2000 event more than lived up to expectations. It was not so much a victory as a rout. (McKlein)

precise technique and his readiness to consider new ideas.

'He's very good at analysing it more like a racing driver would, right the way through from the start of the corner, rather than what may be a side-effect at the end of a corner. He'll break the corner down. It's something obviously we've been trying to get everybody to do for a number of years, but Richard is actually very good at it,' revealed his engineer Simon Cole, an amiable, ex-F3000 racing man usually known within the team as 'Crikey'.

Yet the season had begun inauspiciously. Richard had been very firmly in contention after the first leg of the Monte, only for a cold-start problem to strand him in the mountain town of Gap the next morning. At the time, he was concerned that his demise had presented Mäkinen with victory on a silver platter. In the months ahead, it was some consolation that the sub-zero conditions had caused just as much havoc for Peugeot.

The tyres were somewhat better than they had been in 1999, but tantalisingly, not quite good enough and once again, he was fifth on the Swedish, albeit comfortably ahead of Kankkunen this time.

The Safari could hardly have been more different, not just in terrain, but in its outcome. Richard had been confident anyway, but he could scarcely believe his luck when a plague of punctures cut down the Michelin runners on the rally's first two sections. The two works Subarus were in command by the end of the first leg and their nearest rival was Auriol in another Pirelli-shod car, a Seat. The Safari is still far too long and far too unpredictable to be won easily, however. The fact that Richard claimed his second Kenyan victory in three years was a tribute to his composure.

'It's definitely one of Richard's strengths that he remains very calculated when most drivers would be getting emotional,' Lapworth reflected. 'I think a very good example is in Africa this year, when he scooped up a load of sand and it went in the radiator. He arrived at the end of the stage, he's leading the rally, but his engine is 130° water temperature and he calmly described, step by step, what had happened. He didn't come to the end of the stage and scream on the radio, "The effing engine's overheating and what am I meant to do now?"

'He ran us through it all, so we were much quicker at working out what the problem was and what he should do, than we would have been if we'd spent five minutes trying to calm him down and him screaming at us, "Tell me now!"'

In fact, the engine had got so hot at Elementeita Drift that it had stalled and refused to restart – a development that might have panicked the most easy-going driver. In the end, with the clock ticking remorselessly, the crew managed to restart it by pouring cold water over the engine temperature sensor, fooling it into thinking that the simmering flat-four was ready to run. There was no serious damage done and, unflustered by the knowledge that Kankkunen was tracking his every move, Burns duly recorded his second Safari victory in three years.

If anything, his Portuguese triumph was even more assured, but once again, Richard had made it look easier than it was. Beyond question, the P2000 was instantly, sensationally quick, but it was by no means fully reliable and it tested the

The dutiful father at first, Alex Burns has acquired a taste for rallying and makes occasional but regular outings each year. (McKlein)

driver's ability and resolve to their limits. Two power steering pumps failed in quick succession during the first leg, east of Oporto, and then, as he was cruising back to the city for the night halt, a Toyota service vehicle suddenly veered into his path on the motorway and he rattled the side of the Impreza down the Armco. If his reflexes had been less quick, his rally might easily have ended on the spot, as the rules prevented his mechanics from riding to the rescue outside a designated service area.

Battered but unbeaten, Richard went on the attack the following day, coolly picking off Sainz and Grönholm to regain the lead. He had felt sufficiently confident to ease off on the roughest stretches of the notorious Arganil stages in the bleak hills near the Spanish frontier, but he admitted to a trace of disquiet too, for he knew that the breeze would almost certainly drop at nightfall and that Grönholm would profit from a dust-free run.

If the car was that good what could possibly stand in his way?

Sure enough, to Richard's irritation, the Peugeot man regained the lead that night, but even he regarded it as a loan rather than a gift: Burns and the Subaru were an irresistible force and the following morning, Richard put the result beyond doubt. It had been a hard slog, but a highly convincing victory nonetheless, for the 6.5-second winning margin scarcely hinted at his superiority. He had become the first English driver ever to lead the World Championship and if the car was this good when brand new, what could possibly stand in his path as the season unfolded? He was jubilant, yet far from complacent. His one real fear, he admitted, was Peugeot.

David Lapworth was thrilled and paid due tribute to the driver: 'You can see the way he responds to pressure during the rally. Even in Portugal, there was an element of that. Despite the setbacks, each time he was capable of calculating the pace he needed to go. He wasn't getting exasperated: "No, we can still win this and we can *still* win it." He was under a lot of pressure.'

Two weeks later, second place in Catalonia was a victory of sorts. No one in the Subaru camp had quite liked to say that Pirelli's shortcomings would very probably deny the Impreza drivers a place in the top three, never mind victory, unless it rained heavily. Privately, their expectations were distinctly modest.

In the event, it was wet as the crews left the Costa Brava and Richard instantly grabbed the lead. Even when it dried, the Peugeots were nothing like as serious a threat as expected and the rally became a contest between the Subaru and the Focuses of McRae and Sainz. An electronic glitch that made the P2000 reluctant to change gear cost Richard the lead when the roads dried on the second day, but he nosed in front again when McRae hit clutch trouble and collected a 10-second penalty at the start of the final leg.

Richard had gained an advantage, but not the initiative. Driving immaculately, his fellow Briton retook the lead on the very next stage and, try as he might, Richard was 5.1 seconds down at the finish.

To McRae, there had been no need to prove who was the better driver. To Richard, it was simplistic to compare drivers without comparing cars and tyres. Besides, he had fended off Sainz on his home rally and he had exceeded expectations. If losing a fight to the finish with McRae hurt – no matter what the circumstances – he had no intention of admitting it, but the fact remained that it had been a rare, toe-to-toe clash between the two and for whatever reason, Richard had lost.

Robert Reid is the one man to have co-driven for both, having won the 1988 Hackle Rally, a national event in Scotland, with McRae. He could appreciate the instant attraction of his fellow countryman's style.

'He jumps in the car and goes quick, and that's exactly what he did in the Hackle Rally. I can remember being in Drummond Hill and I knew these stages quite well: fourth gear in an Escort, 80 or 90mph and the windscreen wiper arm started to lift off the screen at his side – it would be a right-hand-drive car – so he just like undid his belt and lent across to see out my side of the screen, without ever lifting going down the quick bit on Drummond Hill and I just thought, "Mm". But it felt really in control and since then, in the early days at Subaru, I actually did quite a bit of testing with Colin as well. Richard, I think it's fair to say, wasn't as impressive the first time I sat with him as Colin was. But, you know who can do it and who can't. Richard's always been "start within your limits, you push the envelope occasionally and come a cropper," rather than Colin or some other Scandinavians, I suppose. It's just what you see is what you get,' he suggested.

As a man who has never taken part in a rally, Lapworth has a slightly different perspective, but he also knows both drivers very well indeed.

'I think what's changed, because Richard's approaching the limit from the other side, is his confidence. I think it was a fairly widely held concern with Richard in the past, "has he got the real killer instinct? Can he really deal with the pressure? Will Richard ever get to the level where you put him head-to-head with Colin McRae or Carlos Sainz on the last couple of stages of a World Championship rally, to take them on?" I think as he's gained confidence, he's got faster and faster – and even then, I can't think of one example of where he suddenly went out and did an amazing stage time. But as he's been tested, what's happened is each time he's been put to the test he's risen to it – never more than he needed to, but he's always risen to just what's required to do the job.

'Even if you take the classic example, Australia in 1999 with Carlos, I still don't think we know how fast he could have gone, because he didn't do any more than he needed to to beat Carlos. I think in the same situation, I wouldn't like to say whether Colin could have gone faster than Richard or not, but I think what you would have seen is that Colin would have been wilder. He would have taken even more

The 2000 Impreza was an instant sensation, Richard taking an accomplished victory in Portugal. (McKlein)

risks than Richard did in order to beat Carlos. Richard seems to have that ability, which is probably a strength, the ability to do just enough and know what is the limit.'

A month later, Richard extended his championship lead to 14 points by conquering a rally that has regularly got the better of McRae: Argentina. Again, it was not straightforward. A succession of minor setbacks, ranging from overheating to a sickly turbo, worn brake pads and a faulty handbrake, prevented him from stamping his authority on the rally from the start, but his pace during the second leg was astounding and he was firmly in the lead on returning to Cordoba that night.

Conditions could hardly have been worse the next morning. Fog and drizzle enveloped the Sierra Grande. As some of the longest and roughest stages lay ahead, Richard was far from out of the woods. Yet despite another bout of overheating, slowing several times to dodge cattle and a puncture on the last corner, he put the opposition to flight on the very first stage of the leg.

McRae retired with a blown engine, the delayed consequence of standing the

Focus on its nose and damaging the sumpguard after a deceptive river crossing the day before. Kankkunen slid off into a wall for a time, while Grönholm and Mäkinen complained bitterly that they had no grip. One look at Burns's time persuaded the Finns that the game was up.

In the prevailing conditions, a moment's loss of concentration could have ended Richard's rally on the spot. Even so, he overshot a junction and slithered into a boulder at one point. The rain was so bad by the last stage that the only way to get the Impreza to steer was to keep the wheels spinning.

As the points piled up, the possibility was raised that the car might be the vital ingredient, rather than the driver. No top competitor will readily concede that the machinery might be getting the results, but Richard was happy to acknowledge that success was owed to a combination of car and driver, and that getting the two to work in unison is an increasingly complicated, intricate process:

'The cars are at such a level now – a very, very similar level – that of course, it's a combination of both. Now, you could say the Subaru's the best car on gravel – but would it be the best car on gravel if someone else was driving it? That much you don't know. Is it the best car on gravel,

In Argentina, Richard and the new Subaru were in a league of their own. The World Championship appeared to be his for the taking. (McKlein)

because the engineers designed it that way or because of the way I set it up? You know it's a very good car, but what's to say if I was driving for Peugeot this year I wouldn't have won in Portugal? You don't know. It's a combination, but it's a combination that runs deeper than "the car is good on that rally and the driver is good on this rally." It runs into how the car is set up and developed with your engineer. It runs deeper than just car/driver.'

Given Subaru's record of four wins in six years, Richard was entitled to approach the Acropolis bursting with anticipation. But the purple patch had come to an end. As the months passed, the drawbacks in the team's bold new design became glaringly apparent, while Peugeot and Ford extracted the full potential from equipment that had benefited from exhaustive development.

On the Acropolis, the Subarus' dampers leaked badly on all but the shortest stages; Burns came off better than Kankkunen, but only to the extent that his car's suspension did not collapse. He still could not lay a glove on the works Focuses. The mechanics worked through the night to devise tougher damper bearings and he was poised to salvage third, only for a blown turbo to pump all the oil out at the start of the final leg. McRae won, but Grönholm did not finish and Richard therefore retained his 14-point championship lead.

New Zealand was just as promising and just as disappointing. Richard was forced to run first on the road on the bone-dry, gravel-caked tracks of the Waikato district during the first leg and was therefore unable to match either Grönholm or his team-mate François Delecour, who could pick a clean – or cleaner – line. Richard crossly asserted that making the championship leader run first was the equivalent of forcing Michael Schumacher to run on a wet track for a third of a Grand Prix.

Then, while Grönholm was running first during the second leg, it rained and a single incorrect tyre choice and a resulting spin prevented Richard from turning the tables. Like McRae, he was still in the reckoning as the last leg began, but he spun on the first stage and then, to the team's consternation, both he and Kankkunen pulled up with the finish almost in sight. The flywheels had shattered. Despite all but rolling the car in fifth gear, Grönholm pulled off a superb victory.

New Zealand promised 100 per cent adrenaline, but mixed it with a large measure of disappointment. (McKlein)

In Finland, no-one expected Grönholm to lose, but Richard did his best to put the matter in doubt. No-one else – not even a sorely disappointed Mäkinen – could hold a candle to the Peugeot man, but Richard was still in touch when he made a tiny misjudgement as he crossed the flying finish of the 11th stage. At Finnish speeds, the consequences were inevitably serious and the car was wrecked in the ensuing 100mph accident.

Richard offered no excuses for his first crash in the best part of two years, but dismissed any suggestion that the pressure was getting under his skin. He had decided that the best way to win the championship was to fight for every point on every rally; if he drove with something in hand, Sainz would almost certainly have been the runner-up in Catalonia and Richard probably would not have been as high as second in Finland. Grönholm pocketed his third win of the season along with the championship lead and McRae, after a cautiously paced rally, claimed second.

Despite hundreds of miles of testing, Cyprus was no better. Once again,

Subaru's shock absorbers were unequal to the strain, this time because the seals wilted in fierce heat, the Mediterranean sun compounded by the lowest speeds in World Rally Championship history; the best drivers struggled to average even 40mph. There were plenty of other problems too, the most serious being a smashed propshaft towards the end of the second leg, when Richard stood at least a chance of finishing second.

'The prop snapped and then I made a big foul-up about two kilometres in. The switches on the dashboard to lock the front differential and to lock it in gear are next to each other and, inadvertently, I hit both, so I carried on in second gear and front-wheel drive, so I'm to blame for half the time loss. So now they're moving the switch,' he said that evening, with admirable self-restraint.

There were more problems during the last leg, including an ECU fault and the discovery that his cool suit had sprung a leak before the first stage. There was no longer any chance of depriving Delecour of third, but he fended off Mäkinen to

Cyprus was a new challenge for almost all the leading drivers. For Richard it was a constant battle against niggling problems of one kind or another. (McKlein)

take fourth and his first points in four months.

The tensions in his relationship with Prodrive had long since become common knowledge. Freed of its wearisome commitment to Alain Prost and Formula 1, Peugeot had money to burn on its rally team and it was not only investing to considerable effect in research and testing, but bidding energetically for drivers. Richard had a contract with Subaru until the end of 2001, but it was inevitable that he would be approached and just as inevitable that he was intrigued.

'Everybody plans for their future. It may be from a sentimental point of view, there's maybe a bit of natural affinity with Peugeot, in that I was around in the days of Des O'Dell and I did receive an awful lot of help. OK, maybe that's a little bit simplistic in the current scheme of things, but I have to think about the car and the team that I have the best chance of winning the World Championship in and I really would like to be in a position to able to choose, and that is something that any competitive person will do,' he explained.

'Say Peugeot come to you and say, "We like your writing, we want you to do all our press releases and we're going to pay you £100,000 a year for the next three years." Are you going to say, "I've got a contract with *Motoring News* for two years and therefore I'll just say, no, thank you very much?" Or are you going to say, "Yeah, that sounds quite good, let's talk about what the possibilities are?" It isn't just money, because clearly they've got the equipment to do it.'

Prodrive had no intention of releasing its only true number one driver and Peugeot turned its attentions elsewhere.

Few forms of motorsport allow the fans to get so close to the action: Cypriot enthusiasts crane to get a better view of Burns and the Subaru in full cry. (McKlein)

A solid fourth place in Corsica closed up the championship battle, but Richard couldn't get on terms with Grönholm's Peugeot team-mates. (McKlein)

There had, no doubt, been pungent words said in private about the P2000's unreliability, but to Richard's way of thinking, he would have failed the team by keeping silent.

'You just want the best every single rally and to see points getting blown away is desperately frustrating. We shout, because if your heart's not in it, then you wouldn't be doing it and your heart is definitely in it, your emotion's in it, it's what you work for. When I make a mistake, like I did in Finland, you know in a week's time you're going to say, "I can't actually do anything about it," but sure, it hits you hard.

'The pressure is definitely on, but it's not just on me. It's on Colin, Carlos and Marcus as well.'

Naturally, he approached the autumn asphalt rallies in Corsica and Italy with a degree of trepidation. Pirelli had worked hard, but Peugeot would certainly be itching for revenge after Catalonia and in Gilles Panizzi and François Delecour, it had two of the world's foremost Tarmac drivers. Beating them in such conditions would be a very tall order indeed.

So it proved, but pretty much the only consolation Richard could draw was that it had proved beyond his championship rivals too. He had beaten Grönholm at least and inched a point nearer in Corsica, when it took a while to adapt to Pirelli's newest, improved rubber, but one of his nightmares came to life in Italy, when he crashed on the Sanremo Rally. It was nothing like his Finnish accident. He had been doing noticeably better than in Corsica, getting closer to Delecour and Panizzi than anyone else until he went a little too fast into a tightening left-hander near the summit of Monte Ceppo and ran wide into a milestone. There was little apparent damage, but the impact was severe enough to twist the sumpguard and, more to the point, to punch a hole in the radiator.

He had gone off about as far from the service area as it was possible to get and the cooling system had run dry long before he limped into Sanremo. Prodrive had even dispatched a van with a tow rope to yank the car from the time control to the service point.

'On a scale of 10 for seriousness, it's about nine and a half,' the Team Manager John Spiller told an inquisitive Sainz as he shooed spectators out of the way and the Impreza barked its way into the control. The engine died in the control itself and the crew had to push it – unaided, as the regulations demand – as far as the tow rope. It never ran again. One of the head gaskets had split.

The car was barely damaged and the crew were completely unharmed, but coming just a fortnight after McRae's much more serious accident in Corsica, in which the Scot smashed his left cheekbone and bruised a lung, it was a reminder that World Championship rallying provides very little margin for error. The one consolation Richard could take was that hitting a milestone was better than plummeting over a drop.

'I have to say I do think it is ridiculous the amount of time they took to get Colin out of that car and I think he's extremely lucky that he wasn't more severely injured or the car wasn't in a foot of water or something,' Richard observed. 'If it brings changes for the better, then at least something good will come out of it, but it does not make me worry.

'If anyone ever complains about the amount of money we get paid for doing this job, go and have a look at Colin's car, go and sit with him in hospital and then tell me that we don't deserve it, because you do get the odd comment from the odd person, "You've got a great job, you've got a great life" – but you are risking quite a lot when you're doing what you do.

'Occasionally you get to the end of like a really long stage and you think, "Well, if a wheel stud had sheared in there, you'd be mincemeat." But I never think it when I'm actually driving, no – I've got enough going on!'

Grönholm flirted with disaster too, hitting a rock on Sanremo's penultimate stage. The impact bent but did not break a suspension link, but he candidly admitted that throughout the final stage, he had been braced for the damaged bolt thread to shear. Yet he beat the Fords and went to Australia with a five-point cushion. Richard's 14-point lead was a distant memory. He would need to win both remaining events. 'Risking quite a lot' threatened to be an understatement.

As the championship headed for a crescendo, Richard kept non-essential commitments to a minimum. But while interviews and PR functions could wait, it was entirely in character that he turned up at MIRA – the test track that might be described as the true heart of the British motor industry – for the final of the Roger Clark Award, which offered a £50,000 prize for a promising British driver. He might have treated budding stars as an irrelevance or as potential rivals, even if they were five or 10 years younger and

Progress has replaced dirt with asphalt, but in other respects the scene would have been much the same in the 1960s or '70s. Richard threads the Subaru through a tiny Italian village above Sanremo. (McKlein)

had a fraction of his experience, but Richard was not only a friend of Richard Stoodley, the scheme's organiser, but had put money into it himself. It was another indication that he felt a sense of duty, quite undimmed by fame and financial reward, to see the sport prosper.

World Championship defeat would be no disgrace. Richard was still the youngest of the title contenders and, given his level of experience, 2000 could be considered his first realistic shot at the crown. The opportunity would come round again. While he conceded that the Impreza P2000's instant superiority had probably raised expectations to an unrealistic degree, just as the Focus's runaway successes had raised Ford's in 1999, the idea of losing the championship after being 14 points ahead was too much to take. Yet after the Rally Australia he had little

Australia is one of the fastest rallies in the World Championship and Richard is in his element hurling his Impreza down narrow, treacherously slippery forest tracks. (McKlein)

choice but to accept that it was not only possible, but likely.

Richard found himself in the highly unusual position of being disappointed to gain a place in the results – and of being accused of unsportsmanlike behaviour.

In Australia, gravel was not so much a consideration as an obsession. Western

Australia's forest tracks are covered in a notoriously persistent layer of small stones akin to ball bearings. Running first was such a handicap that, some years before, the most cunning drivers had started hanging back towards the end of each day, knowing that they would be re-seeded in position order and that sacrificing a few seconds would be amply repaid the following day when their more impetuous rivals had ploughed the gravel for them.

The organisers realised that the road surface was beginning to distort the entire nature of the contest and had applied for a waiver from seeding custom in 1999. Under the alternative system, the fastest

competitors could choose their re-start positions and therefore had no incentive to drive slowly. It had shown promise, but there were shortcomings too and as the manufacturers were unable to agree upon a modified version for 2000, the FIA refused to grant a fresh waiver.

It was to be expected that two of the three days would be spent jockeying for position, much like a long-distance athletics race, but not that it would degenerate into a slanging match as increasingly controversial tactics were employed and the stewards were called upon to exclude well-known competitors or change the results after every leg.

Five drivers were in the running for the world title when the rally began. By the last leg, there were three at most: Grönholm, who was the rally leader, Burns and Mäkinen, as McRae had been eliminated by a blown engine and Sainz was excluded for stopping in a control area.

Service points become mobile command posts. When the cars are on stage, teams can maintain radio contact with the drivers and analyse data collected from previous stages. (McKlein)

Richard was inexorably sucked into the controversy. Fortuitously – a charitable interpretation – Mäkinen jumped the start of the critical stage in the second leg that would determine re-start positions for the final leg. Prodrive personnel were on hand and instantly demanded to know if Mäkinen had left early. Keeping to the organisers' brief, the marshal said that he had not. It wasn't until the following morning that his championship rivals learned that Mitsubishi's man had gained a 10-second penalty that conveniently dropped him to third, with a fraction less gravel to plough.

Prodrive calculated that a place on the road was worth between 10 and 15 seconds. There was a championship at stake. Richard got a puncture at the start of the last day's first stage. In line with established procedure he was given time to change it, forcing Mäkinen to run in front. His rivals were beside themselves with fury, unable or unwilling to accept that this had turned into a bare-knuckle contest – or at least that anyone else should force the rules so flagrantly.

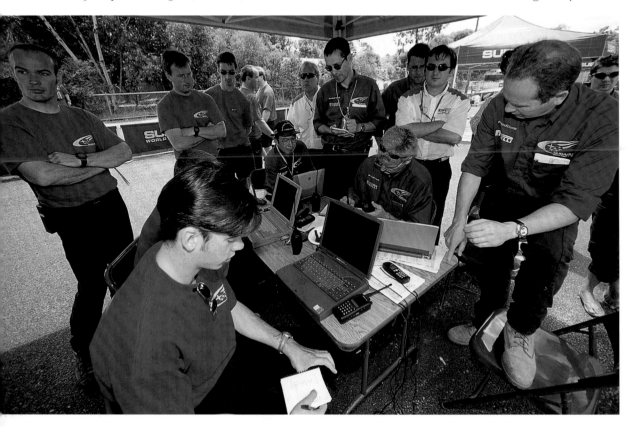

'I hate Richard,' Grönholm almost shouted as he unwound himself from his 206.

Television footage gave him some support, for it suggested that the Subaru crew had deflated the tyre themselves and while there was no conclusive evidence, the puncture seemed contrived in a way that jumping the start had not. Pirelli staff were plainly uneasy and there was unsubstantiated talk that Burns might be summoned to explain himself to the stewards.

There was no summons, but Richard was no more at ease than the Pirelli men. Worse still, once tactical considerations were shoved aside in the sprint for the finish, his Impreza's handling failed to inspire confidence and the engine was below par. There was no question of holding Mäkinen, but it was near-impossible to reel in Grönholm either, despite the notional advantage of running third rather than first. Perhaps, as Mäkinen suggested, the gravel was so deep that it took more than three cars to disperse it. Perhaps Grönholm had surpassed himself

in setting the stage times he did; Richard was certainly impressed. Perhaps the Impreza failed to rise to the occasion.

Nine-tenths of a second divided the Peugeot and the Subaru before the last, 1.7-mile stage, all of which had been used and therefore swept of gravel. Richard drove faultlessly. For the first time, he took the steepling downhill jumps towards the finish in sixth gear. Grönholm lurched into a messy slide on an early corner and admitted that he thought he had lost. Yet he gained 1.8 seconds. It was enough to give him second place, by 2.7 seconds, and ease the pressure as he headed for Richard's territory.

For his one remaining rival, there was also the thought that different tactics might have paid off. He had been 40 seconds ahead midway through the second leg and just possibly he might have defied every expectation and won from the front. As it was, he reckoned that his World Championship prospects were 'slim,' even

At this stage there was everything still to play for. (McKlein)

before Australia sprang its final surprise.

The scrutineers had noticed something unusual about the Mitsubishi's turbo and a post-rally inspection revealed that it lacked the specified water-cooling system. Mäkinen was thrown out and Grönholm was proclaimed the winner, increasing his lead from seven to nine points. Even if Richard won in Britain, fifth place would make the Peugeot man World Champion.

Before their home round, the Rally of Great Britain, even Colin McRae all but conceded that Richard was the favourite. Everything from tyre supplier to the championship incentive made the Subaru man the better prospect in his view.

But Richard was feeling the heat. He had got a real taste of the kind of adulation and pressure that McRae had first encountered five years previously. Every time he stopped during the recce in Wales, fans would appear at the Subaru's door, asking questions, urging him on, and sometimes even offering to make sure that Grönholm would not see the finish. It was a little hard to handle – especially the offer to sabotage his rival – and he gently pointed out that he has to compete in Finland too.

His final flourish was a remarkable achievement

After two stages, Richard had slumped to 21st place and his chances of winning the rally, far less the championship, looked in tatters. He was less than a mile from the start of the St Gwynno stage, 20 miles north of Cardiff, when he misinterpreted a pace note and cut the Impreza across the apex of the first rather than the second corner in a sequence. He realised his error in an instant but couldn't jink the car back on to the road before the left-rear wheel caught something unyielding in the ditch. He crabbed his way out of the stage with the loss of 30 seconds and, as if to emphasise the scale of his error, his new team-mate Petter Solberg took the lead.

When he pulled the wheel off, Richard found that he had smashed the suspension out of line. More seriously, he had cracked the hub. If he could straighten the suspension he ought not to lose too much more time, but the hub might fail at any moment and he still had two more stages to attempt before service. Sure enough, while he set a good time on Tyle, the wheel bearing collapsed two miles from the end of Rheola 1 and he conceded another 30 seconds and he still had a further 45 miles to cover before getting to the service area in Builth Wells. If he could only do that, he was convinced that he retained a fighting chance of winning the rally and therefore a sliver of hope of becoming World Champion.

He lashed the hub together with the spare wheel retaining strap and limped north. Although reduced to no more than 25mph as the hub loosened, he reached the time control. As he admitted, he had been very lucky, but that evening his chances of winning remained slender. He had fought his way back to fifth, in spite of a spin on the fifth stage, but he had made no real headway against McRae, the new leader, or even Grönholm, who had startled his opponents by taking the lead for a time. Pirelli's advantage over Michelin had evidently disappeared.

The opening stages of the second leg would be crucial. Richard could dispose of the likes of Mäkinen, Sainz and probably even Grönholm soon enough, but he had to exert pressure on McRae if he was going to win. The signs were not good: he was up to third after one stage and reeling in Grönholm hand over fist as stage records tumbled, but McRae was quickest on the first stage, lost only a fraction on the second and gained a little more on the third. Both the British drivers were revelling in the battle and quite clearly, McRae wanted not just to win, but to crush Burns.

'I can't go an awful lot faster. That's a good speed, but if Colin's doing the same speed it means he's also taking risks, which is good,' Richard commented.

For his part, McRae reckoned he could go a little more quickly if he needed to, but after another stage Richard's assessment looked closer to the mark. Rheola was in a poor state having been used the day before and when Colin turned into a rutted right-hander near the start, the sumpguard crashed out and the Focus flipped into a ditch, punching a hole in the radiator. McRae's rally ended two miles later when he had no choice but to switch off rather than destroy the engine. Richard was entitled to regard this as revenge for Catalonia.

Grönholm was the leader once more, but only by three seconds and it was Peugeot's turn to feel uneasy. A Burns victory had suddenly become more than likely, and it was vital that their driver recognised the fact and rejected the temptation to give the home favourite a run for his money.

It would have suited Richard down to the ground if Grönholm had picked up the gauntlet, but he never betrayed a hint of nerves and his Peugeot never missed a beat. Richard swept into the lead at last on the 13th of the 17 stages, in spite of throttling back.

The final day of the rally was a matter of staying out of trouble and praying for a miracle. The fans were out in force, people standing at the roadside in Welsh hamlets holding placards reading 'Go Burns go' and Richard did his very best to meet their expectations. He clinched his fourth win of the season, but it was not enough to claim the title. Grönholm was second and Richard was therefore five points short.

It was plain enough that he was pleased rather than thrilled, but he insisted that losing the championship was no longer a disappointment.

'I said I felt before the rally that it was kind of over anyway – there was still a lot of hype, but it was really over before we started. I can say that now, because of what's happened, but that's the feeling I

One slight misjudgement looked as if it might jeopardise Richard's chances of a hat-trick on home ground. Assisted by Robert Reid, he endeavours to keep the Subaru running. (McKlein)

Mud and rain are meat and drink to a top rally driver. Richard heads for victory on the Rally of Great Britain. (McKlein)

had to have inside me. If I had the feeling that I had to win for the championship, it would have been too much pressure to be thinking about that the whole time. I was just thinking to win the rally,' he said.

'Winning feels very different, I guess because of what's happened with the championship. In some ways, because of what happened with Colin. I don't want to rub salt into the wound, but I was pushing very hard and I was the only one to take any time off Colin when he was running strongly and I don't know, if I wasn't there, then maybe he wouldn't have had to be pushing so hard. He said just before he went off that he had a few per cent in reserve, but it shows.'

He offered no excuses for the season as a whole.

'We started to go downhill after Argentina. The speed has been there generally, but not always the reliability. I've also made some mistakes, in Sanremo and

in Finland, but it's 14 rallies and we've had a pretty dismal run up till now and Australia – we've had two fourth places or something, which is a bit steady to be winning a World Championship.

'Marcus has proved all year that he can cope with a lot of pressure. He's had a better year than me and he's made fewer mistakes than me. There is no question he deserves to win the World Championship.'

It had been an honourable defeat and his final flourish was a remarkable achievement. The RAC Rally was first held in 1932 and yet Richard had become the first British driver to score a hat-trick, and only the third of any nationality. On a rally held in such thoroughly unpredictable conditions, that spoke volumes for his skill and judgement.

'In many ways, it's been a development year with our car and hopefully that will go towards our new car and reliability will be better,' he concluded.

He would just about have time to catch his breath. The new Impreza, the 44S, urgently needed testing. The Monte Carlo Rally beckoned.

Richard Burns: results

Abbreviations

TS	Talbot Sunbeam
TC	Toyota Corolla GT
FE	Ford Escort
205	Peugeot 205GTI
309	Peugeot 309GTI
911	Porsche 911
SLN	Subaru Legacy Group N
SIA	Subaru Impreza Group A
SIN	Subaru Impreza Group N
ML	Mitsubishi Lancer Evo III
MC	Mitsubishi Carisma GT
SI98	Subaru Impreza WRC98
SI99	Subaru Impreza WRC99
SI00	Subaru Impreza P2000
RS2	Ford Escort RS2000
SLA	Subaru Legacy Group A

1989

	Panaround	30th
13 May	Mid-Wales FE	12th
	Millbrook	11th
	Severn Valley FE	DNF
Jul	Kayel Graphics TC	DNF
Oct	Cambrian	14th

1990

	Panaround 205	30th
	Imber 205	DNF
	Donington race 205	5th
	Dukeries 205	12th
	Croft rallycross 205	1st
	Border 205	33rd
7–9 Sep	Flanders 205	25th
20 Oct	Audi Sport 205	16th
25–28 Nov	RAC 309	28th

1991

2 Feb	Wyedean 205	11th
22–24 Feb	Talkland 205	DNF
15–17 Mar	Ardennes 205	class win
4–5 May	Welsh 205	13th
12 May	Mid-Wales Stages 309	3rd
9 Jun	Dukeries 205	15th
6 Jul	Kayel Graphics 205	7th
18 Aug	Border SLN	3rd
30 Aug	Cumbria SLN	DNF
11–13 Sep	Manx Int 309	class win
18–19 Oct	Audi Sport 205	11th
24–27 Nov	RAC 309	16th

1992

25 Jan	Mazda Winter SLN	2nd
21 Mar	Vauxhall Sport SLN	DNF
4 Apr	Pirelli SLN	41st
11 Apr	Granite City SLN	8th
18 Apr	Imber 911	3rd
16 May	Manx Nat SLN	DNF
13–15 Jun	Scottish SLN	10th
20 Jun	Severn Valley SLN	1st
26 Jul	Loton hillclimb RS2	2nd
8 Aug	Kayel Graphics SLN	2nd
26 Sep	Rally Car Stages SLN	3rd
24–25 Oct	Elonex 309	11th
22–25 Nov	RAC 309	DNF

1993

20–21 Mar	Vauxhall Sport SLA	1st
17–18 Apr	Pirelli SLA	1st
4–6 Jun	Scottish SLA	1st
30–31 Jul	Ulster SLA	DNF
15–17 Sep	Manx Int SLA	1st
21–24 Nov	RAC SLA	7th
3–6 Dec	Thailand SLA	2nd

1994

31 Mar–3 Apr	Safari SIN	5th
17–19 Jun	Indonesia SIA	DNF
29–31 Jul	NZ SIA	DNF
13–15 Aug	Malaysia SIA	2nd
16–19 Sep	Australia SIA	5th
22–28 Oct	Hong Kong–Peking SIA	2nd
20–23 Nov	RAC SIA	DNF
3–5 Dec	Thailand SIA	2nd

1995

8–10 Mar	Portugal SIA	7th
13–16 Apr	Safari SIN	DNF
27–30 Jul	NZ SIA	DNF
14–20 Oct	Hong Kong–Peking SIA	3rd
19–22 Nov	RAC SIA	3rd
2–4 Dec	Thailand SIA	3rd

1996

3–4 Mar	Thailand ML	DNF
10–12 May	Indonesia ML	DNF
15–17 Jun	Malaysia ML	2nd
4–6 Jul	Argentina ML	4th
27–30 Jul	NZ ML	1st
13–16 Sep	Australia ML	5th
19–25 Oct	Hong Kong–Peking ML	2nd
4–6 Nov	Catalonia ML	DNF

1997

1–3 Mar	Safari MC	2nd
23–26 Mar	Portugal MC	DNF
21–24 May	Argentina MC	DNF
8–10 Jun	Acropolis MC	4th
2–5 Aug	NZ MC	4th
19–21 Sep	Indonesia MC	4th
1–3 Nov	Australia MC	4th
23–25 Nov	RAC MC	4th

1998

19–21 Jan	Monte Carlo MC	5th
6–8 Feb	Swedish MC	15th
28 Feb–2 Mar	Safari MC	1st
23–26 Mar	Portugal MC	4th
20–22 Apr	Catalonia MC	4th
4–6 May	Corsica MC	DNF
20–23 May	Argentina MC	4th
7–9 Jun	Acropolis MC	DNF
24–27 Jul	NZ MC	9th
21–23 Aug	Finland MC	5th
12–14 Oct	Sanremo MC	7th
5–8 Nov	Australia MC	DNF
22–24 Nov	Britain MC	1st

1999

17–20 Jan	Monte Carlo SI98	8th
12–14 Feb	Swedish SI98	5th
25–28 Feb	Safari SI98	DNF
21–24 Mar	Portugal SI98	4th
19–24 Apr	Catalonia SI98	5th
7–9 May	Corsica SI99	7th
22–25 May	Argentina SI99	2nd
6–9 Jun	Acropolis SI99	1st
15–18 Jul	NZ SI99	DNF
20–22 Aug	Finland SI99	2nd
16–19 Sep	China SI99	2nd
11–13 Oct	Sanremo SI99	DNF
4–7 Nov	Australia SI99	1st
21–23 Nov	Britain SI99	1st

2000

20–22 Jan	Monte Carlo SI99	DNF
11–13 Feb	Swedish SI99	4th
25–27 Feb	Safari SI99	1st
Mar	Portugal SI00	1st
31 Mar–2 Apr	Catalonia SI00	2nd
11–14 May	Argentina SI00	1st
9–11 Jun	Acropolis SI00	DNF
13–16 Jul	NZ SI00	DNF
18–20 Aug	Finland SI00	DNF
7–10 Sep	Cyprus SI00	4th
29 Sep–1 Oct	Corsica SI00	4th
17–23 Oct	Sanremo SI00	DNF
9–12 Nov	Australia SI00	2nd
23–26 Nov	Great Britain SI00	1st

Index

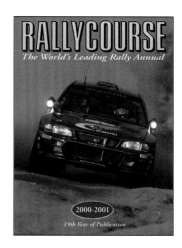

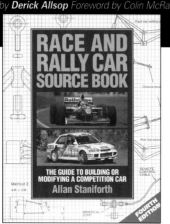

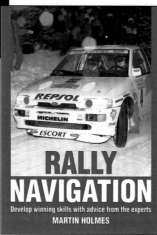

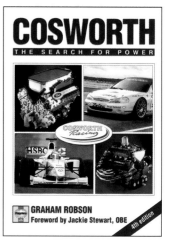

Other titles of interest